PARENTS
ON THE MOVE!

PREPARING YOUR FAMILY FOR A SUCCESSFUL
AND CREATIVE RELOCATION

KATHLEEN MCANEAR SMITH

DESTINY IMAGE™ EUROPE srl
Via Maiella, 1
66020 San Giovanni Teatino (Ch) – Italy

"Changing the world, one book at a time."

This book and all other Destiny Imagetm Europe books are available at Christian bookstores and distributors worldwide.

To order products, or for any other correspondence:

DESTINY IMAGE™ EUROPE srl
Via Acquacorrente, 6
65123 - Pescara - Italy
Tel. +39 085 4716623 - Fax: +39 085 9431270
E-mail: info@eurodestinyimage.com
Or reach us on the Internet: www.eurodestinyimage.com

ISBN: 978-88-89127-88-96-4
For Worldwide Distribution, Printed in the U.S.A.
1 2 3 4 5 6 7 / 14 13 12 11 10

Making Kids a Relocation Priority

(CNN)—Traveling overseas for business is one thing, relocating overseas for work is another matter.

If you are moving abroad, one of the biggest concerns is your family, especially children and their education.

"More corporations are realizing it is too expensive to have a corporate assignment fail because of their children's education needs," Kathleen Cocklin [McAnear] from education consultants Childtrack told CNN.

Firms have taken note since the Global Relocation Trend Survey report in 2001 found that 40 percent of overseas postings fail mainly because of family concerns.

Yet making the move overseas a success for you and your children is all about planning, experts say.

"It is wonderful when families move happily, usually they are the ones who have done the most preparation," says Cocklin.

"Two days should be spent actually in the classroom (overseas). It does not take more than a week to do your survey trip, if you have done your homework beforehand."

The biggest question is whether children should follow the system back home, join an international school, enroll in a local one or sign up for distance-learning from home.

The expert's advice is to know your child and their needs and make sure the transition to the next destination is as smooth as possible.

"If you keep track of your children, then you have an idea of their learning pattern," says Cocklin.

"You can go ahead to the next school and say 'this is how the last experience has been' and connect the new teacher with the old teacher via e-mail."

Cocklin also advises families to think about the long-term strategy, since promotion or moving to a different company can shift the family back home or to a new destination—each with its unique schooling system and set of problems.

When children move, not all fit in. They may be behind in class or find the social change difficult, leading to a loss in confidence that affects the child's learning and happiness, believes Cocklin. Families should focus on the positive points they have learned from being overseas, she says.

"The strengths would be—rock solid geography; a knowledge of another country, learning about different food and ways of living," she explains.

"On return, your children are going to be ahead of the others who have never been anywhere and never intended to travel overseas."

—CNN's *Meara Erdozain*
http://www.cnn.nl/2004/TRAVEL/02/12/biz.trav.expat.family/index.html

DEDICATION

This book is dedicated in loving memory to my father, Frank E. McAnear…it's a long way from Arkansas!

Acknowledgments

⸻◆⸻

Years ago I was teaching what the English call "Reception" class in Prince's Mead school in Winchester, England. One morning a young American mother, Joanne Babbitt, came to my classroom. She introduced me to her son John, and his younger brother Andrew. David, her husband, just started working in a bank in London, and she was about to accept a senior position with Chase Manhattan, Europe.

I spent that year helping John adjust to being the only American child in a totally English classroom. Andrew, however, grew up with two sets of vocabulary (English and American) and his transition would come later when the family moved back to the New York area. It was Joanne and David's idea for me to be their education consultant, and as I enjoyed the challenge, they recommended me to other parents. We often joked that their kitchen table became the unofficial U.S. Headquarters of Childtrack, a small British (that was official) education consultancy to the families of senior bankers. I am not sure when the business started growing, but soon I gave up my day job teaching school and began serving Chase Manhattan, Lehman, and JP Morgan families. I wish to thank the Babbitt family for their love and support, and for their guest room during those New York business trips in the early days of birthing Childtrack Ltd. They kept it real.

I wish to acknowledge and thank a very special group of women who assisted in the growth and development of Childtrack, which is the foundation of this book. I call them "The Founding Mothers." Though restricted from sharing our Christian faith with clients, they gave their all in praying for children to be placed in the right schools all over the world. Gay Mallam, Terri Koche, Joanne Clarke, and Sally Chow laid the foundation of our service as followers of Jesus. They used their expertise in cross-cultural transition, business administration, teaching, biblical knowledge, and in the godly wisdom of being mothers themselves. They gave way too much for me to simply say thank you, so I say instead that I "give thanks" for all they did in serving global family life in the name of Jesus. I thank Sally's husband, Ping Chow, for his patience in reviewing our first business plans. From the very beginning of our friendship, I gave—and still give—thanks for Marlene Cantor who dared to believe that I, a school teacher, could step out and run a business. Thank you for believing in this work even before it began.

There are so many people to thank for those years of running Child-track, from Karen Kaldezar of the former PKL Relocation Company in London, to the headmasters and headmistresses of many schools, some of whose stories you will find in these pages. I give thanks that many of you have encouraged me to write *Parents on the Move!*

I give thanks for Bob Gormley, a young pastorate leader at Holy Trinity Brompton Church, to whom I passed on Childtrack when, after ten years of running the business, I left to get married and moved out to the English countryside. When they talk about "business angels," Bob was and is that for Childtrack.

I give thanks for my children, Angela and Mark, and what I call their "traveling courage." Oh the trust of young children as they head off to see grandma and granddad in South Korea, say good-bye (mid-year) to friends in America, and slip back into English classrooms at the start of a new term! Now that they are grown and take off on their own adventures, I give thanks for all they taught me in being a global parent. I give thanks for Angela's work as a university psychology student writing our literature review as well as contributing valued information on the impact of corporate assignments from a child's point of view. I give thanks for the many times my son came and sorted out computer organization and looked at the technical side of what we had to do!

My new step-children, all adults and starting their own young families, have made a valued contribution to the work of this book. I especially thank Alison for introducing me to another generation of expats in Italy, raising families and trying to make sense of global parenting in post 9-11 times.

I give thanks for my husband, Christopher, without whom this book would never have been written. He believed in this project, and prayer covered me every step of the way. His business expertise enabled me to have a clearer focus on how I could get years of serving global families into a format that was both practical and useful. His love and support made writing possible.

A word of thanks and admiration has to go to my mother. At 88 years of age, she is still boarding planes and traveling to another country to see a grandchild get married. She knows all about missionary global living, from being a sister to a life-long Southern Baptist missionary and in taking off at 77 with my dad to live and work in South Korea. You are my inspiration! I also give thanks for my brother and sister who have listened to so many of my stories of life overseas and somehow always welcomed me home.

I give thanks for Destiny Image Europe. Though I had been encouraged by others to write this book for the secular side of Wall Street and Canary Wharf, the very first time I prayed with the Destiny Image Europe production team I knew I had made the right choice to not compromise in giving God the glory for *Parents on the Move!* Thank you, Florian (New Writers Outreach), for recommending my writing to the publisher. Thank you, Marzia, for your gift of encouragement in every area of project management. You are a sister in Christ! Thank you, Angela, for your excellent standards in editing; any mistakes are definitely mine! Thank you, Pietro, for being "Papà!" to the whole team and taking a risk on a first book from this writer.

Above all I wish to give thanks to Jesus. He is my Brother who welcomed me back to the Father and taught me how to not just listen, but to obey the still, small voice of the Holy Spirit. I said this book was for You, Jesus, to honor Your teaching. Each morning when I began writing I said, "This is Your book, may anything that is just of me be edited, and what is of You go deep into the hearts of readers." I pray that now. I give thanks for all the Father has taught me and given me the privilege to pass on to you.

ENDORSEMENTS

———◆◆✦◆◆———

Kathy's book is an excellent resource for anyone uprooting their family and moving. She brings together practical advice, experience, and wisdom that is priceless in what can be a very unnerving time. This book is like having a friend alongside, who has walked the path, to point out the hurdles you may face. Moving overseas is an adventure, but there are often situations when you wish you would have had someone tell you how to navigate. Kathy offers this advice—firsthand experience, wisdom, and good old common sense!

Cath Taylor
Ellel Ministries USA
www.ellelministries.org

I give this book the highest stamp of approval—from the perspective of a Jewish mother who also happens to run a world renowned education consultancy for relocating families. It is choc-full of all the information that "about-to-be" expats need to know, from locating a home to finding the right school, to spousal assistance and seeking emotional support. Filled with compelling anecdotes, *Parents on the Move!* is an easy read, but also provides detailed steps—a thorough how-to guide—to every aspect of the relocation. Although intended for a Christian audience, *Parents on the Move!* is a book that every potential expat as well as seasoned expats will finish with the peace of mind that only comes with the realization that "I can do that."

Elizabeth Perelstein
President, School Choice International
www.schoolchoiceintl.com

Parents on the Move! is a real testimony to Kathy's trust in God and reflects her belief that He is always sovereign and good. I found the book very educational on a number of levels. It gave me real insight to what families go through moving from one culture to another. This book is filled with lots of wisdom and heaps of practical advice, as well as an emotional and humorous read—a really good blend as this book is about issues where emotions can be highly charged. It was brilliant to include points about children with special needs as so often they are forgotten during times as these. Kathy's priority on faith and family is excellent and will help couples more easily talk about the issues; the examples raise topics that may be or have been problems. *Parents on the Move!* encourages communication between husbands and wives and older children.

Jane Tooher
Women's Pastor, St. Peter's Barge
Canary Wharf, London
www.stpetersbarge.org

This book is a gem as it helps parents handle things without panicking. My husband is a senior manager in one of the largest mineral companies in the world. Several years ago when the children were tiny, we made eight full house moves in three countries over a period of five years. Big life decisions are needed from us just when we least expect them, and temporary overseas moves for families often fall into this category.

Kathleen reinforces the importance of seeking guidance (spiritually and practically). She shares her extensive knowledge and professional experience, as she has successfully worked in the relocation industry for years. There is an invaluable section for parents to analyze what their current lifestyle and key values are, and very helpful sections about how to find the right schools—the essential first piece in the relocation jigsaw puzzle. Kathleen's true-life examples from other parents and her own personal stories are touching and relevant. At last! A comprehensive book that HR departments can provide families as they anticipate their move.

Kathryn Eghan
Mother of three
Corporate assignments to Pakistan, Dubhai

I LOVE IT! The style is accessible and friendly and downright useful. I want copies of this to show my students how to write this kind of how-to book based on your own experience and case studies. It is beautifully written.

Jo Parfitt
Author, *A Career in Your Suitcase*
www.expatrollercoaster.com

But seek first His Kingdom and His righteousness and all these things will be added to you as well (Matthew 6:33).

…including airline tickets, the right schools, temporary accommodations, a house or apartment, a family-friendly neighborhood, a friend or two, cell phone, computer connection, the perfect babysitter…

CONTENTS

FOREWORD

Moving is never easy—moving with a family can be even harder. Moving abroad with a family? This ranks right up there with a root canal on the torture spectrum. Between the hours of packing, the good-byes, the hunt for a new place to call home, schools for the children, making new friends, and the total loss of the familiar...it's enough to make anyone throw up his or her hands and declare, "I'M STAYING PUT!"

But ideally life is about moving forward, adjusting to change, and accepting that God's plan for you may be different from what you had always imagined for yourself and your family. The reality in these trying economic times is that "staying put" is fast becoming a luxury. Many of us have no choice but to go where the jobs are. Once you've accepted this reality, parent, what do you do? Pray and read this book. Read this book and pray. Either way, make sure you do both!

Kathleen McAnear Smith's *Parents on the Move!* is equal parts testimonial, road map, and how-to guide. Kathleen has seen it, lived it, and is all too eager to share the wisdom she's gleaned in her more than 30 years living as an expatriate and her decade as an education consultant for senior investment bankers. Since moving from the United States to the United Kingdom, she has helped several thousand families understand, embrace, and appreciate change.

"Life in the wild world of relocation, especially overseas relocation, can be overwhelming," Kathleen, a veteran globetrotter, points out. "Priorities seem to fly out the window the moment you see the whites of the e-tickets." This book of hers ensures that this doesn't happen. Nearly 60 percent of corporate assignees are relocating with children, and unfortunately 30-40 percent of these assignments end in failure, largely because of family concerns. The wisdom in her book ensures this doesn't happen to you and your loved ones.

Kathleen eschews lofty, esoteric talk and instead shares her knowledge with readers in a refreshingly, straightforward style. She is as warm as she is honest, as empathetic as she is pragmatic. "Rock solid priorities enable successful moves," she writes. "Rock solid priorities stand firm in the face of Human Resource departments, realtors, and even education consultants declaring they will tell you the 'must have priority list' for your next move." Kathleen's priority list is simple: faith, family, and friends. For an orderly and fruitful transition, those 3Fs must be inextricably linked, she believes. After reading this book, you will certainly be inclined to agree.

Parents, Kathleen knows that having faith doesn't mean that you won't have questions. You will have dozens upon dozens. How do you deal with the loss that you inevitably feel when you relocate overseas or even locally? Does God want you to go? How do you find the perfect school for your child? How do you make new friends? How deeply do you want to assimilate? How much of your national identity do you want to keep? Drawing from the Bible, her own experiences, and those of people she's encountered over the years, Kathleen provides detailed answers to all of the above, and she deftly tackles issues as complex as birthing children abroad, home schooling, and establishing a dedicated support system.

The Bible, she is careful to illustrate, is packed with true accounts of relocation and is chock-full of advice about how to handle these monumental events. Seek first the Kingdom of God, and then all else will be added, says Matthew 6:33. "…If your Presence does not go with us, do not send us up from here" (Exodus 33:15). These are just some of the many verses used throughout to remind you of God's counsel for people on the move. "He always has a plan," she writes. "A key factor in the success of that plan, as in any area of your life, is obedience to His direction."

One of the other most important keys to a successful relocation is establishing a personal support team. I am a living testament to just how paramount this is. Nearly 40 years ago, my parents left their homeland of Nigeria and emigrated to the United States in search of an education and economic prosperity. They were in their early 20s, and like many immigrants who flock to the US, they were short on money and long on dreams. Leaving all they had known was difficult, making a home in this new country even more so.

All that changed when Kathleen's parents, Frank and Libby McAnear (evidence that angels do indeed walk among us) entered into my parents' lives. The McAnears met my parents at the First Baptist Church in Washington, D.C. and immediately welcomed them into their lives and their home. They were their surrogate parents, their confidantes, and their biggest cheerleaders. They prayed with them and for them, attended their graduations, and watched over my younger brother and me when mom and dad needed a well-earned break. In turn, my parents came to regard the McAnears and their three children as family.

Decades later, that remains unchanged. With all that she's juggling, Kathleen still finds time to pray for my family. My parents speak with her mother regularly (her father has since passed) and continue to ask that God watch over the McAnears and their loved ones. Though many miles separate us all, our bond stretches across waters and beyond borders.

Saying good-bye can be difficult. *Parents on the Move!* makes saying hello to your new life abroad much easier.

Lola Ogunnaike

PREFACE

"Why is that man so resistant to living a year in Paris!" a young Human Resources person said to me when discussing a new employee being sent to their European headquarters. "I'd jump at the chance!"

In the end, this particular employee and accompanying family loved their year in Paris, but when planning their relocation, the resistance stemmed from finding a school for their 15-year-old son. They wondered how they could be good parents in a foreign city.

In these challenging economic times many parents, having never thought of moving even across town, are considering a major family move to secure employment. Many are simply "going where the jobs are."

Whether you have lived worldwide or even if you have never ventured far from home, *Parents on the Move!* will guide you through the myriad of details and decisions that will make for a successful research trip that focuses on selecting schools for your children and connecting to communities that nurture what you value in life.

Though written for Judeo-Christian families, every potential expatriate (expat) can benefit from focusing on family while living in what I call the wild world of corporate, diplomatic, military, missionary, or non-government organization (NGO) work assignments.

Some employers or sponsors are fairly good at identifying and giving the support you need for a successful family move. They understand that when you are married and have children, relocation is altogether different from the days when you flung a backpack over your shoulder and headed wherever the wind took you. According to 2009 Brookfield's Global Relocation Survey, over 60 percent of expats heading out to the wide world these days are married, and approximately 50 percent have children accompany them.[1]

If your Human Resources (HR) Department has recommended this book to you, then they know that relocation with children is a world away from "single assignments" where networking after hours ranked higher on your to-do list than checking out a nursery school.

While nearly 30 percent of all corporate expatriate assignments end in an early return or even failure,[2] few companies are happy to budget for aborted assignments. Assignments can end early for excellent reasons, but concern arises when the reason has nothing to do with the work at hand and everything to do with family adjustment and children's education. To the work assignment manager, failure means an employee is giving up and heading home before the assignment is completed. There is little or no return on their investment.[3]

I've written this book to help families fulfill their obligations to each other, the employer, and to their future memories of a successful time in a foreign country, or even a different region of their own country.

Introduction

As a parent, failure is when your family is not thriving where it is planted. Global Trends reports that approximately 90 percent of relocation resistance issues (not wanting new assignment) are due to "family concerns,"[1] including: children's education, family adjustment, and spouse resistance. Resistance?

One family, who was quite reluctant to move from Chicago to London was thrilled to learn that despite one of their children having severe special needs, they could do more than just live in "survival mode" while the breadwinner worked every hour possible. They learned that their home country wasn't the only place that provided outstanding care and resources. The father said to me, "This is the first time in seven years—since our daughter was born with this disability—that I've seen a light in my wife's eyes. Sometimes it helps to see how another country deals with this issue."

Sometimes, as this father said, but not always. Fortunately, a successful relocation is not dependent on location, and some of the happiest expats are in places that may never be featured on the top ten tourist locations. A successful international move is about meeting your family's needs and keeping on track toward the goals you have for your family. It is about nurturing what you value in life, and thriving in a new regional or even international setting.

When interviewed on a CNN Business Traveller program in 2004, I said that moving to different areas gives children "rock solid geography." I still believe that, but even more importantly, I think that my own children as well as others who have had the privilege of traveling and living with their family in other regions and countries have grown in rock solid values. In fact, values have been tried and tested in the international arena for thousands of years.

Ever since Adam and Eve left home, God has been alongside people as they discover new places to live and work. I want to share with you the impact that God has had on my life with over 30 years of living overseas. A relocation support spouse myself, a parent as well as schoolteacher, former Peace Corps Volunteer, and founder of the original Childtrack Education Ltd consultancy to the banking community in London, I will share with you a way of developing a strategy that works for your family. This strategy helps you collect the information you need to make successful decisions regarding schools for your children as well as establishing an appropriate support team for family life.

You are offered hard-won information gleaned from many years of living the expatriate life. Whatever part you play in this growing global nomadic community, you will enjoy the straight talk about how to successfully relocate with your family.

Chapter One

STRATEGIC PRIORITIES

The relocation team filed into the boardroom at a major London bank. There we were—the relocation team leader, the estate agent ("realtor" in American English), the Human Resource administrator for the bank, and me—the American education consultant.

We had been told to prepare a five-minute presentation, outlining our proposal for assisting an American senior banker and his family in their move to London. As we sat at the huge mahogany table, the doors closed behind us.

We shuffled our papers and had slightly nervous chitchat. The man we were about to meet was famous for not wasting time, and he was on his way straight from the "red-eye," the overnight New York-London flight. He might not suffer presentations easily, I decided. I put away my five-point talk to simply listen.

Suddenly the door flew open and our Wall Street banker bounded into the room. Almost bouncing on his toes, he quickly pointed around the table.

"Which one of you is the education consultant?" he demanded.

I put up a hand and looked straight at him, waiting to see what he would say next.

"You," he smiled, "if you do your job, then the rest of these people around the table have a job. Otherwise, you might as well pack up and go home."

"Then shall we get started right now?" I asked.

"Absolutely!" he said, and finally sat down at the head of the table.

"May I ask you some questions about your children?" I was quite aware of the other relocation professionals at the table. My consultations with parents are usually private and confidential.

"Fire away," he said smiling again. "Want to see photos? My wife packed photos." His hand was already pulling photos from his wallet and he placed three beautiful pictures on the table in front of me; then he proudly placed a whole family photo on the table.

I admired his obvious love for his family and proffered several questions while quickly taking notes. Ten minutes later, I had enough information to get started on the school search; in fact, I had just the school in mind. As the meeting started to focus on other issues, I excused myself and went out into the hallway to start phoning school admissions' staff.

This man had a clear priority—his children.

Who Gets to Set Priorities?

It is really great when people say they put their family first, but it can be rare to see it in action in any high-energy, goal-oriented world. From corporate life to military assignments, to non-governmental projects to missionary lifestyles, people are exhaustingly busy. Many people would *like* to make their family a priority, but maybe husbands, wives, or kids can only *dream* about being a priority because of the realities of a busy family life.

How can you set priorities and make them work? When there is a world to save, or a market target to meet, who gets a break to focus on their family? Who gets to live out their priorities and what do you have to do to know which ones are the right ones? *Should* your family be first on the list? Work? Church? God?

What about the concept of work-life balance? If you've just learned that your factory is closing, your team in Wall Street is being transferred to Hong Kong, or you and your family were accepted to work on a mission in Asia, life in the wild world of relocation, especially overseas relocation, can be overwhelming. Priorities seem to fly out the window the moment you see the whites of the e-tickets.

PRIORITY CHALLENGERS

Maybe now that the economic climate seems out of control (or at least your control!) you are for the first time considering moving to find a job. Maybe you have been told that your department is closing and you have no choice but to relocate. Maybe you have moved before, but there are just so many unknowns in these challenging and changing times that it is all you can do not to be anxious. Economic uncertainty coupled with spreading terrorist threats could make you feel more like running for cover rather than seizing an opportunity for work in a new or unknown location.

It takes a strong person to make the decision to declare, once and for all, the priorities that will act as a plumb line for major life decisions. It takes a very strong person to live out these priorities especially when it comes to family moves, whether overseas or to another region or city. It's far easier to say you'll get around to figuring out those important priorities once the move is over, once the "dust is settled." You can justify thinking this is a little theoretical for a time when you need to be packing boxes and figuring out how to tell the coach that your daughter won't be on the soccer team next September.

And yet, *rock solid priorities enable successful moves*, no matter which airport, country, or city you live in for the next five minutes. Rock solid priorities stand firm in the face of Human Resource departments, realtors, and even education consultants declaring they will tell you the "must have priority list" for your next move.

You do not have to be pulled in every direction. *Be ready* for people to come out of the woodwork, telling stories about "when I lived in Bahrain," or Madrid, Seoul, Surrey, Westport, or Atlanta. You must set your own priorities when planning your relocation.

You can have priorities that meet your family's needs and enable success in every aspect of an overseas or even an out-of-town assignment. Priorities that work for any relocation need to be set—and that's what the remainder of this chapter is all about.

THE PRIORITY LIST

Let's be real about this list. The world can pretend that it's "all about you." That's great for the marketing department, but I have never met a successful global nomad who believed it. As a result of living an overseas life myself for over 30 years and running an education consultancy for senior investment bankers for ten years, let me show you what I found works best.

By listening or reading the news, you may be hard pressed to believe anybody lives by these priorities, but here is the priority list that works:

- Faith
- Family
- Friends

Later we will look at friends—low maintenance or otherwise—but in this chapter we will look at faith and family. *All of us* operate out of our belief system or even "systems!" You may not be able to discuss this at the office, but you can at least be honest with yourself. You are going to be making many, many decisions that affect your life and the lives of your spouse and children, so why not take a moment even if it is just the moments you get while waiting for the plane or the dentist, to check the basis for your decision-making.

Faith—Priority #1

It has been my experience, from working with several thousand families over many years, that families of faith have a smoother transition from one region or country to the next. It is about hearing and seeing answered prayers, but also the fact that a faith family moves from one part of their faith community to another.

It has been my great pleasure to spend time at the Saint John's Wood Synagogue in London, going with New York Jewish families on the synagogue tour as they discuss the family support provided in that community. It has been a delight as Caroline, the head of the synagogue's nursery school, has welcomed children of all faiths and made families feel welcome. There is something about the loving support of the faith community that is missing in secular society.

The Bible says that we are to seek first the Kingdom of God, and then all else will be added (see Matthew 6:33). The Bible does not say, "except when taking on an international assignment," or "except when moving your family to Seattle."

Our Father God loves a good move!

If there ever was a practical guide on how to relocate, it's the Holy Bible. We have a God who gets into minute detail when it comes to moving His people, and we have the Holy Spirit to guide us and open our hearts to His Word. His Word speaks directly to our circumstances.

In Scripture, we have the benefit of reading true accounts of families moving from one land to another again and again. From Moses organizing a mass move that would make relocating a corporate division look like a Sunday picnic, to Paul training the next generation on how to live while on the road, we have evidence of Father God wanting to be intimately involved in your family's relocation. He wants to be in the details!

Take some time to read the stories listed below to raise your faith as you are reminded of God's power and provision for people on the move. As you wonder about the decisions you need to make and ponder what to do first, you will see He always has a plan. You will see that a key factor in the success of that plan, as in any area of your life, is obedience to His direction.

- Genesis 12—God tells Abraham to go

- Genesis 30:25-36—Sometimes leaving is a little tricky!

- Genesis 45—Talk about relocating in difficult economic times; an encouragement to have a good attitude as you travel

- Exodus 13—God is your route planner

- Numbers 13—The details of a research trip

- Ezra 8—Now here's a travel journal!

- Joshua 19—New location boundaries, details

- Ruth 1—Re-entry issues and moving to a new land

- Luke 2—Mary and Joseph relocate

- Matthew 4:12-17—Jesus relocates

These passages confirm that Father God has long been in the details of relocating His people. My prayer is that we remember the example of Moses when he said to the Father, "If You are pleased with me, teach Me your ways so that I may know You and continue to find favor with You." The Lord reassured him that His presence would go with Moses, even giving him rest in his travels. Moses then gave the all-time great response to a relocation call,

"If Your Presence does not go with us, do not send us up from here" (Exod. 33:13,15).

Seeking His Kingdom way of doing things is the beginning of bringing order to your relocation.

"Order my footsteps, Lord," is your whispered daily prayer as you gather the children and pack your bags.

"Order my footsteps, Lord," is your silent prayer as you hold your baby, board the plane, and hope you don't lose your laptop.

"Order my footsteps, Lord," as you watch your teenagers consider new schools.

"Order my footsteps, Lord," as your mother kisses her only grandchild good-bye until Christmas.

"Order my footsteps, Lord," as you leave your job and become your husband's entire support team in a new land.

"Order my footsteps, Lord," as you try out a new language.

"Order my footsteps, Lord," as you close the front door and lock it for the last time.

Many years ago in the United States there was an ad that said, "Don't make a move without calling Smith!" (No relation!) I suggest that you don't make a move without checking Jeremiah 33:3. This verse is often called God's telephone number. God says, "Call to Me, and I will answer you and tell you great and unsearchable things you do not know."

Don't know where to begin with this, your first out of town, regional, or overseas move? Even if you are like my mother-in-law on her 21st military move, God will answer you. When He is the beginning of your relocation strategy, success will always follow.

Faith Steps

Faith Step 1: Does God want you to go?

As I was driving along the lovely Connecticut road one morning, I was reflecting on how grateful I was for the schools my children attended, the school where I was teaching, and the friends we all had made during the four years we had lived in Ridgefield.

Though my children are half English and half American, I was originally from a southern American family, and I hadn't been terribly confident about getting to know northern American life. Yet after only a few years of living in this beautiful part of the world, I was praising God for some of my closest friends and (very important to me) walking partners. I could live in Connecticut forever!

Just before I pulled into the driveway and parked the car, something nudged me to give all this joy back to God, and say, "Lord, if You want us to move back to England, then I am willing…I think."

That last bit was my sinking heart feeling that the Holy Spirit was asking something from me that I wasn't totally prepared to do. Father God was preparing my heart, it seems.

Within five hours, we heard the announcement that IBM would be moving us once again to the United Kingdom.

The first Faith Step is to give all relocations to Father God.

In the Book of Exodus, it says, "In all the travels of the Israelites, whenever the cloud lifted from above the tabernacle, they would set out; but if the cloud did not lift they did not set out—until the day it lifted" (Exod. 40:36-37).

If you have called on His name, and asked if He wants you to relocate, ask Father God for "a cloud." OK, so you don't have to necessarily stand in the back yard and wait for the skywriters to spell it out for you, but ask Him for personal guidance from the Holy Spirit. Ask Him to give you clarity that He wants you to move to another part of the country or world.

Just because your company, the government, or missionary society thinks it's a great idea to move your family, doesn't necessarily mean it is His idea. Unless you are military and are obeying orders that you have sworn allegiance to follow, say to those involved that you need some time to think about this decision.

Even if you only have 24 hours before a response is required, God is capable of letting you know what He wants you to do. After all, He knew how much time you would have to consider accepting an assignment before you even asked.

Faith Step 2: Check the peace

I was not a happy camper that day in Connecticut mentioned in Step 1. I had firmly pitched my tent in my country of origin, and with young children I was soaking in every minute of raising them in America.

As a school teacher, I had great summer holidays and my son was enjoying running around our big house and playing at the nearby pond. He was learning to fish, and in the winter he and his sister tried ice skating on that same beautiful pond. We had BBQs in summer evenings. Family members including grandma and granddad, aunts, uncles, and cousins all came and visited us. Going north of the Mason Dixon line was an experience for them; but oh so much cheaper than a trans-Atlantic flight!

The idea of getting three quotes for shipping our stuff back overseas again was not giving me much joy. Still, I knew in my "knower" that Father God had this move in His plan for our family. I may not have been pleased about going, but I had solid peace knowing it was His move.

Check that you have the peace of the Lord for any assignment that you accept. If you do not have that peace, ask for more time to consider the relocation. Only when you have that "peace that passes understanding" can you call on Him to help you adjust your attitude and begin to attend to the practical details.

If Father God is directing your relocation, you can depend on Him to know and meet the desires of your heart. He knows the best new school for your children. He knows which church will have a dynamic youth group that is even now praying for a drummer for the worship band and will welcome your son! He knows which house is being prepared for you, and the insights you will gain from living in a new neighborhood.

God knows all about your move, and can't wait to show you how He is going to be with you. When you have His peace, from your obedience to His call, He will be the One who helps you know what to pack, and how to tell the kids the news. He will be the One who helps you cradle the baby on the long-haul flight.

He will be the One who gives you a knowing peace about selecting a new school, and provide school placements where space seems impossible.

He will be the One to comfort your mother and provide creative ideas for keeping the family connected. He will be the One who sees the two of you, husband and wife, as one, and will teach you how to support each other in a new location.

He will be the One who finds you new work and opens doors to understanding aspects of who you are in Christ that He knew you were too busy to see at home! He will be the One who supernaturally enables you to learn a new language and be with you as you shop in a foreign place.

He will be with you as you close the door at your house for the last time, and will be standing there waiting for you as you unlock the door of your new home.

Faith Step 3: Parents are the decision-makers

Families are a gift from God. As parents, Father God has given you responsibility for raising your children and making certain decisions on their behalf. Often well-meaning parents give their children inappropriate responsibility when it comes to making a decision regarding whether or not a family relocates.

It never ceases to amaze me how children truly believe it is their fault if things go wrong while on overseas assignment. One of my "client kids" had his first failure on a spelling test the very day his dad came home and said that the project he was working on was closing and he was being offered another position in yet another country. Though mom and dad were actually quite excited about the move, that 6-year-old somehow thought that his spelling test failure was the cause of the upheaval that ensued.

With especially young children, parents need to be clear that the decision to move is yours and not theirs. If for any reason the assignment ends early or even extends, your children need the assurance that where you live and work is your responsibility, not theirs.

To preserve childhood in children, let there be little responsibility for little shoulders. They will have enough to deal with learning how to be the new kid on the playground.

Older children may be included in discussions about potential moves; but remember that these discussions can be unsettling. Teenagers tend to withdraw from friendships when they think or feel there is the possibility of leaving, even if the move is not for another year or so.

Once you have accepted an assignment, older children need to be involved in school and church selections. It does not mean they have the deciding vote, but their preferences need to be heard.

This is a time for practicing your listening skills.

Put a couple of Family Listening Nights on the calendar, and try out the Family Relocation Listening Exercises found in Appendix A. If life is a little too crazy in the days leading up to the move, these exercises are great long-haul flight conversations!

Family—Priority #2

Sixty percent of corporate assignees are relocating with children these days. The sad news is that in some years, as many as 40 percent (some years 30) of all overseas assignments end in failure. Many would argue that only 4 percent of aborted assignments constitute any corporate definition of failure, but for whichever definition, whichever figure you use for early termination of an assignment, 90 percent of assignments that are cut short for unhappy reasons, usually due to family concerns, especially regarding education and school selection.[1]

Your children do not need this stress and neither do you. Classroom teachers are often bewildered by the impact. Marriage counselors can be challenged by breakdown in the international arena; and, by the way, your company does not budget for little return on its investment.

His Family

If Father God has told your family to go, then He will be with you. This is one of His many promises. But before you say, "yes, next?" know this: He wants to guide you at a level and with such detail that you may never have experienced. There is a type of move that is just right for you, at this time and stage of your family life.

In Chapter 2, I want you to consider a faith-based strategy that has helped many families make quick and accurate choices regarding their relocation. It's simple, fun, and will save you loads of time and frustration. Using the Seven Levels of Moving insights, you can select the level of move that is just right for your family.

You and your family *can* have a successful relocation.

Chapter Two

SEVEN LEVELS OF MOVING

YOUR SUCCESS IS HIS GLORY

Our office received a telephone call from one of our Manhattan clients, whom I will call Dana. Dana was a successful attorney, and she had decided to take a year off work to accompany her husband on a one-year assignment to his corporate headquarters in London.

They had a six-year-old daughter, whose school places would be held for her while she was away. They also had a new baby.

"This is a great way to spend maternity leave!" said this energetic mother. She would enjoy the focus of planning a research trip.

"OK. We arrive on Sunday. The schedule says that we look around neighborhoods on Monday and visit the schools on Tuesday and Wednesday."

"That's right," I said, "It's an eight A.M. start, and I'll meet you in the hotel lobby."

There was a momentary silence, and then this highly competent lawyer asked, "Would you mind being right there when the elevator door opens?"

We both burst out laughing and I said, "Not a problem!"

We had previously discussed that with work and the children, it had been a long time since she had traveled above 125th Street, never mind getting on a plane and heading out over the Atlantic. She could use a little handholding, at least until she was used to jumping back and forth between Manhattan and London.

For now, this detail-oriented young woman was thinking more about the numbering of the floors in United Kingdom (UK) houses and buildings as it was different from the United States. With a tight schedule, she would prefer to not spend 20 minutes looking for me, especially, as she said, "with the meter running."

Dana's husband's company had given them a one-week, all-expenses-paid research trip with the purpose of selecting a neighborhood, house, and school for the kids—all within that week. Good economy or difficult economy, the company relocation package was not a top business priority; and if a family needed longer, it would be out of their personal pockets.

The children were staying with grandma while Dana and her husband flew off to make major decisions within the given time frame. Dana reckoned, quite rightly as it turned out, that her husband would end up in meetings at his new London office and leave many of the arrangements to her. She, however, was on a mission to make this relocation a great experience for her family. Dana was prepared to do the planning and preparation and make the research trip a success.

She read the recommended book list[1] and then spent time considering the Seven Levels of Relocation detailed in this chapter. Dana used the Seven Levels as a tool for narrowing down the overwhelming amount of information available. She read through the Level Descriptions, which gave her and her husband talking points for revealing what was in their hearts and minds for their family. She knew that if they were obedient to how God wanted them to live, He would give them the desires of their hearts.

Still, in their case, Dana and her husband found it difficult to discern whether or not their family should relocate at Level Two (stay with American schools but travel extensively throughout the host country and region) or at Level Six (immersing as much as possible into host country culture).

Dana and I set up a School Visiting Schedule that would give her insights as to which relocation level was right for her children. We prayed that God would open doors and close doors. We prayed for divine appointments at schools that would give clarity to Father God's plan and purpose for their relocation. Dana knew that God had a family adventure in mind that would lead to learning more about themselves as well as the Father's heart for their family life.

TOOL FOR COLLECTING INFORMATION

The Seven Levels of Relocation is a tool developed especially to assist families as they deal with the huge amount of information needed to make high-impact decisions when moving overseas.

As you pack up your home in one country and settle into another, there is too much information for any one person to handle effectively. Through reflecting on the level of relocation that is appropriate for you and your family, you will narrow down both the type and the amount of information you need to collect to make decisions regarding three key areas:

1. Selecting school or schools for your children.

2. Selecting a home and neighborhood.

3. Selecting a family support network.

RELOCATION LEVELS

A Relocation Level is the level at which you and your family become part of any given community. Each of the Seven Levels of Relocation has to do with cultural dominancy. To select a level that is best for you and your family, you will need to take a moment to reflect on just how much of your own national culture and faith culture you want around you, and how much of any new culture you are willing to absorb into your family life.

One of my closest friends, Marlene, is Jewish. When she first moved to Connecticut, she said it seemed quite strange to live among so many Christians in her new town.

"What do you mean?" I asked.

"Well, I miss some of the delis, and the Hanukah cards, or having a large synagogue for the kids to go to Sunday School."

She didn't feel any prejudice against Jews, but noticed the town had a different feel to it in that life didn't revolve around the Jewish calendar.

"I think I know a little of that feeling," I said. "In the Bible-belt where I'm from originally, there are large Christian book stores, and I miss the gas station attendant asking me if I'm saved!"

While this example is fairly light-hearted, you need to be aware that in some communities being a person of faith is a high-level risk. In some parts of the world, you need to truly keep your head down if you are not of the dominant faith group. Cultural dominancy is all about which culture gets a say in how we live in a given community. As you read through the levels of moving into another culture, ask yourself, "How much do I want to fit in?"

Even if you choose to live as a Baptist in an Anglican world, or a Brethren in a Catholic community, or a Christian in a Muslim world, there are national cultures to consider when you relocate overseas. As this book is written primarily for Christian families, or those of Judeo-Christian heritage, it is assumed that your core values are based on Scripture and that fact will not be changing wherever in the world you live. This book is for parents who choose to pass on their faith family values to the next generation, but who at the same time need to look at decisions regarding how much of your nationality culture you want to hold on to while living far from home.

Families who have lived all over the world and have had children born in several locations will recognize a level of relocation that does not have any one national culture defining how or where they live. Yet, people who have lived most of their lives in one country need to reflect on how much of their own national culture they are willing to leave behind and take on aspects of another. Have a look at the following questions before you read through the Seven Level of Moving—and let the family discussion begin!

QUESTIONS FOR THE ENTIRE FAMILY

1. Do I have a dominant national culture? For example, can you say, "I am Swiss or American, or British?" Or do you have two cultures such as Italian-American? Some people may have two or three passports, but they were raised only knowing one national culture.

2. If you can define, or simply label your national culture, do you want it to dominate how life is lived, including holidays and classroom traditions?

3. How deep do you want to go into another culture? For example, are you excited about learning another language or the traditions of another nation, or are you at a time in your life when you have had enough of living overseas and would rather make your home an oasis of your national traditions?

4. How much of your own national culture do you will wish to pass on to your children? This question is important for every member of the family. It's not just about having certain items for your baby, or the nursery rhyme collection from home, or the yellow school bus, or sports, or the senior prom, or graduation ceremonies. It's all about shared experiences that define a culture.

Looking at your own culture and considering just how dominate you would like it to be in the life of your family determines the level you wish to live in any new region or country. There are no right or wrong answers to these questions. This is a time for you to get to know yourself a little better, recognize the desires of other family members, and then to give your hearts and minds to Father God who will confirm His plan of action.

Affects of Timing

Timing can influence your choice of level of relocation. There are times in many people's lives when an international relocation may not seem like the best timing for your children, even if at other times you would have jumped at the chance.

One of my American clients, whom I'll call Dan, and his wife Susan, lived in Japan for five years. They had one nursery school-age child who was born while they were in Tokyo, and they were now expecting their second child. They both thought it might be a good idea to head home for at least a year or two.

They longed to be with their wider family back in Chicago; as it happened, the company agreed that the project in Tokyo was coming to a natural end. It would be good timing for the husband to return to the home office.

There was an excitement in the air about going home, and Susan was happy to order the packing boxes. There were phone calls back and forth to the States in anticipation of their child being born in the same hospital where Susan had been born. Susan's mother was just putting the finishing touches on the welcome party that would greet this young couple at O'Hare airport. Three days before Dan was to sign his new work contract, the company said he was needed in London and he could not go to Chicago. Susan nearly shouted, "But I'm halfway through reading Robin Pascoe's 'Homeward Bound!'" But she controlled herself.

Anyone with any experience in global assignments has heard stories such as this. With Dan so quickly rising in the company, they decided to accept the London assignment; but this highly traveled couple made a deliberate choice of making this move a Level One relocation.

They selected an American-style nursery school, moved into an almost totally American neighborhood, with wide American-sized sidewalks (for power stroller walking), and chose an American church and American women's club for social support. These young parents may not have headed home, but they got as close to it as possible. Experience had taught them that when having a baby, they wanted extra support to ensure a successful work assignment.

WHICH LEVEL IS BEST?

Often a husband or wife want to make a different level of move than their spouse, and have to come to some sort of compromise. Looking at these levels brings clarity to your discussions about the type of neighborhood, schools, and church that supports the spiritual growth of your family while far from home.

In recognizing the type of move you would like for your family, you can collect the information you need, not just pile up brochures or overload on Websites. Knowing the level of relocation you *consider appropriate* for your family will identify adjustments that need to be made as you settle into your host country. Knowing the level of relocation *that is possible* in your new location allows you to reflect on any necessary cultural adjustments and whether or not you are comfortable with those adjustments. The *best level* of relocation is the one where you and your family have agreement and you can see God's confirmation.

WHO GETS TO REFLECT?

Reflecting on which aspects of relocation are within your comfort zone and which are not can be a luxury. Knowing who you are and what you want in the whirlwind of a corporate, diplomatic, or even missionary move can be an "Oh God, help me!" moment. My mother-in-law who has made 21 military moves said that the evacuation out of Egypt was an epiphany moment for her. God gave her certain clarity as to who she was as she loaded two small children, one recovering from measles, onto the cargo plane headed for Cyprus—clarity, yes, but not a lot of options. Her only choice was her attitude.

You may not know exactly where you are going or even why, but if you know that you *are* going or *meant* to go, look at each level of relocation and take time to seek God's wisdom on which aspects of this relocation are part of His plan and purpose for your life at this time.

DESCRIPTIONS OF THE SEVEN LEVELS

Pray before you read through the descriptions of the Levels of Relocation. Ask Father God for His Holy Spirit to reveal to you the Level that is right for you at this time in your family life. Try not to discuss your preference with your family members until everyone of appropriate age has had a chance to read these descriptions for themselves. Remember that the level of relocation is a decision for parents, though you will want to know what your children believe God is saying to them. Listen carefully to each other, and agree that while parents have the responsibility for decisions about moving, you will be looking to Father God for confirmation for all the family in the details of your move.

Experience

As you consider these levels, keep in mind that there are Levels of Experience as well as Levels of Relocation. For example, you may have only Level One in experience, but want to relocate at a Level 3 or 4. Whenever the Experience Level and the Relocation Level do not match, let this be an indicator that you may require longer-term assistance as you settle into your new location. We will discuss this more at the end of the chapter.

Level One

What does Level One relocation look like?

The Family: This level describes a family in which all members have the same passport and you have only one country's passport. You do not wish to adapt to another culture, or at least keep any adaptations to a minimum. You want to be surrounded by people and places that allow your own nationality values to dominate conversations, choices, and actions.

As human beings, we act out of our belief systems; and people who choose a Level One relocation do not want to negotiate their everyday lives under the power or authority of another nationality's belief system. They want to pass on their own nationality values to their children, at least in their children's early years.

A family that selects a Level One Relocation wants to operate as much as possible within the bounds of their own cultural norms.

Level One Schools: You want to send your children to a school where most of the other pupils are from your own country and features your home-country curriculum and education values. If you are American, you will want to check that the school celebrates Thanksgiving and teaches your children American history. If you are English living in New York or Buenos Aires, you will want to check that the English school will keep you up-to-date with the English National Curriculum and will, of course, remember the fifth of November!

The long-term education goal for families that prefer a Level One Relocation is to eventually head back to your home-base country; if that includes planning to attend college or university, you hope your kids will want to attend a home-based college or university. You are hoping that their overseas experience will give your kids the edge over "the competition" when it comes to college entrance!

Level One Community: You choose to live in a community that is dominated by your own culture. You prefer to have your own nationality as neighbors. If you cannot find your nationality group in your new location and this is important to you, consider whether or not this relocation is for you or how to find new friends, especially for the non-employed spouse.

Level One Social Support: You choose to attend a place of worship where the congregation consists mostly of your own nationality. You are happy to join clubs and social activities especially designed for your nationality. For Level One Relocation, you want to meet people from your home country as much as possible, even if it is just to commiserate. People who choose a Level One Relocation often head home for the major holidays, but can find it fun to meet up with local expatriates for days such as the Fourth of July for Americans or Bastille Day for the French.

Dinner Party Test: When you invite people for dinner, everyone will be from your own nationality and you will serve or order "food and drink from home."

Level One Experience Level: You have absolutely no experience in moving or living overseas with or without your family. You may have traveled to far away places while on vacation, but you have never lived in another country.

Level Two

The Family: This level describes "one passport families" but often includes "two passport families." Level Two Relocation is when, as parents, you and your spouse hold two different country's passports, but have made a decision to raise your children in one culture and select schools that support that culture. You may be, in fact, a two passport family, but you act and live as a one passport family. Everyone in your family speaks the same language, even if it is a second language for either you or your spouse. You want to explore your new location, or host county culture, but from the launch pad of one culture.

Level Two Schools: You will select schools that have a majority of pupils from your country and teach your home country curriculum and values. You will want to check that the holidays from home are celebrated, though you are happy if the school focuses on learning about host country customs and traditions. You want to get to know your host country, but prefer to see what is important according to your nationality group. This is geography and social studies going live! Your long-term education goal for your children is to get your kids to focus on the colleges or training programs back home. You are hoping this experience overseas will not only give them a competitive edge over other applicants, but will have broadened their education and mindset.

Level Two Community: You will want to ask your housing advisor to find a neighborhood that has "other Americans" or other "French people," etc. Though you want to explore your host country, you would prefer to do it from the filter of your own nationality's community. If you are moving to a major city, you are hoping there will be shops nearby that sell food from home.

Level Two Social Support: Though most of your friends are from your home country, you actively seek information about places of interest in your host country, and may even have a host country friend who has lived in your home country and tells you they loved your country. You still want to worship at home country churches or synagogues if they are convenient, but are happy to join a local congregation if there is plenty of your own nationality in attendance. Any social clubs you join will be especially for your nationality, such as the American Women's Club or an American Men's Golf Club.

Dinner Party Test: You invite people from your own nationality and might include one or two host-country people who have lived in your country, as long as you know they will not say anything critical of your country. You will be serving "back home cooking."

Experience Level: You may have relocated within your own country and even have lived overseas before, but you always chose to live, work and socialize within the bounds of your own culture.

Level Three

The Family: This level describes a one or two passport family looking forward to being part of the international community. Your children are growing up as third culture kids,[2] and you value that they will have other friends who are also "dual nationals." Even if you are a one-passport family, you want your children to know how to live comfortably with other nationalities.

Level Three Schools: You want to send your children to an international school and where possible, will consider the International Baccalaureate as the curriculum of preference rather than any home or host country curriculum. If you choose to home school, the world is literally your classroom. Your long-term education goals for your children include a hope that they will head to the home country for further education, though you will understand if they have "caught the travel bug," and at least look at universities or training programs in another country or two.

Level Three Community: You want to find an international neighborhood and steer away from living in areas dominated by any one national cultural group.

Level Three Social Support: You want to join a church or synagogue that has a large proportion of members from a variety of countries, but you tend to find yourself spending time with your own nationality, albeit your internationally-minded countrymen. While you may drift toward your own kind, one of your values is that the world is a better place because of the variety of nationalities. (Level One families may have this value too, but they don't want to live with them.)

Dinner Party Test: You find it a relief from international living to invite internationally minded expatriates and compare notes with other mothers hunting down Bisquik/Marmite/Bagels. From time to time, you will also want to invite people of other nationalities who at least sympathize with your own culture's way of doing things. You are aware of major world events and often solve all of the world's problems over dinner. If you serve wine, the wine's origin will depend on your dinner guests—South African? Californian? French? Australian? Chilean, etc.

Experience Level: You have traveled overseas with your family once or twice before and know that you may not be heading home after this move.

Level Four

The Family: This level describes a two or more passport family; in fact, your family likes to collect passports almost as a hobby. You may be a child of dual nationality parents yourself, and though you know *where* you were born, you find it difficult to even think about having only one country as "yours."

At this level, you are totally immersed in international living. If this is you, you have quite an eclectic mix when it comes to family traditions. If you are into celebrations, you name it, and you will celebrate! As you have friends in just about every time zone, New Year's Eve is quite an occasion.

Level Four Schools: You are happiest with your children studying the International Baccalaureate curriculum in an international school. If you choose to home school, the world is your classroom. The long-term education goals for families that select a Level Four Relocation often include a preference for your children to choose advanced study from a worldwide range of opportunities. Your children may travel for a year or so before deciding where to attend college or for further training. These children often do well remaining in the international arena for additional education, as they are more comfortable in multicultural education environments. Most international schools, but not all, are located in cities; but whether they are in city or countryside, all international schools provide a social network of families from around the world for you to enjoy.

Level Four Community: As international as possible! You choose to live in an international community, and steer away from living in areas dominated by any one national cultural group. Inform your relocation agent that you do not want to live in your own nationality community, if there is one.

Level Four Social Support: You prefer to join a church or synagogue that has a large proportion of members from a variety of countries. You prefer to join international clubs or societies. You do not join clubs representing just one nationality group, and any social group you decide to join will inevitably need to have the word "international" in the title or be known for members attending from all around the world. Selecting a church in London or New York, for example, is easy at Level Four, as the flow of global nomads is never ending. Finding a support network for someone who prefers to relocate at Level Four in a small town, in any country, is more difficult.

It is a wise use of your research trip to connect with someone who is experienced in helping people settle into new communities. In every part of the world, there are relocation companies dedicated to introducing you to their country. Take time to have a chat with someone who can give you a cultural orientation as well as someone who can assist you in selecting a new house or school. Though they may look well-traveled and highly experienced in international living, Level Four people need real help when making a move. They can sniff cultural dominancy a mile away and it can be difficult for them to adjust to living at other Levels of Relocation.

Dinner Party Test: You are happiest if there are a variety of nationalities around your table. The "more nationalities the merrier" is your motto as you discuss world issues over a glass of very good wine, though country of origin (wine or people) is irrelevant. You do not believe that any one national culture has the answer to life's questions (only your faith does that for you).

There is a core value for living in "the international zone." It is often most obvious in people who select a Level Four Relocation. If you select this level, it may be in no small part because you value saying what you like about your own country (or countries) but you do not criticize someone else's country. You may not agree with the politics or values of another culture but you are sensitive to show respect for what other people may be going through when having to watch the news from home. You watch world news on more than one channel (the national bias of many news channels is irritating to you) so that you can keep up with events that could affect people you know and love.

Level Four people do not assume that they can ridicule another culture and that the people around the table agree. You occasionally may state documented facts about another culture or even say that when you were in a particular city, for example, you had an experience that led you to believe something about that culture, but a Level Four person would never say "All Americans…" Or "All English people…" They understand that stereotypes are not helpful when it comes to living peacefully as possible with others. If you prefer a Level Four Relocation, you want to be around other people who share this value.

Almost unknowingly you will monitor sermons at church or talks at conferences for whatever you define as "cultural bias," though others listening to the same sermon or speech won't even register what was said. You invite people to your home from all nationalities and, quite frankly, hardly have a clue as to where they are from. The greater the nationality or language mix around your table the happier you are. You may not want to invite people who have been "out two minutes" from their own country unless you are ready to reconcile yourself to an evening of Level One or Two conversations, but you *will definitely not* invite someone twice who thinks that ridiculing another country counts as humor.

Experience Level: You have moved overseas with your family several times and prefer to think that living in different countries is just part of global family life these days.

Level Five

The Family: You are a one or two passport family. While you prefer to be part of the international community in that you may live in an international neighborhood, your children attend international schools and you join international churches and social groups. *Your focus is on getting to know your host country and its internationally minded people.* You may attend family and work events in a variety of countries, but you tend to vacation in places recommended by host country friends. You take time to see the world via your host country eyes, and even prefer their news channel!

There is a leaning toward celebrating host country holidays that happens almost without noticing. "It's just easier." As many mothers have said to me, "I often forget when we used to celebrate things in our last country. I just see the reminders in the store here and go along with whatever the children are celebrating at school."

Level Five Schools: People who prefer to relocate at Level Five know they are not staying forever in the host country and select international schools so that their children can be with teachers who understand global nomadic life. The way that they focus on the host country is by simply avoiding their own nationality at the international school gatherings and looking for every opportunity to get to know host country people. You even prefer a few host country teachers in the international school. Your long-term education goal for your children is to head home, but you would also support your children choosing a host country for college or university.

Level Five Community: You may live in an international community simply because you are living in a major international city, but you seek out host country neighbors. You prefer a neighborhood where there is a majority of host country people, while still having a reasonable commute for the kids to their international school. Whether you are moving to England or China, you are hoping that your kids will make local friends, even if your children are attending an international school for the sake of academic continuity.

Level Five Social Support: While you support the activities of your children's international school, you may want to have your family attend a host country place of worship and gain membership in host country clubs. You seek out host country nationals who have lived overseas themselves. In your desire to meet as many host country people as possible, you steer away from anyone from your own nationality who happens to belong to these groups.

Dinner Party Test: You invite people from a variety of nationalities, including your own home country provided they have lived in the host country for considerable time, but you prefer the internationally minded local people. You couldn't care less if your dinner party guests like your country of origin or not and consider that robust conversations about international living is part of living overseas.

Level Six—A and B

There are two types of Level Six. Type A is for families living in a major international city (City Six). Type B is for families preferring to relocate to the countryside (Countryside Six). Type A and B are two different relocation experiences, though you will make the same type of choices when it comes to schools, neighborhoods, and social support network. Your purpose for relocating may be to start or develop a business, and to do that you must get to know the local people. Or you may have married into a new culture and find that you need to live in an area where a Level Six Relocation is the only choice. Missionaries often choose this level of living in a host country.

The Family: While Level Six families hold anywhere from one to quite a number of passports, usually two-passport families select this level of relocation, often relocating to a country that is country-of-origin for one of the family members. Level Six is all about total immersion into the culture of another country, whatever your country of origin.

Level Six Schools: Level Six schools are host country schools. With regard to your long-term education goals for your children, you may select this level of schooling for your children if you prefer to have your children (eventually) have the option to attend the host country further education provision. Take great care when totally immersing a child into a local culture with the intention of pulling them out to "send them home" at a later date. A local school may be excellent for your children's early years, but make a conscious decision regarding long-term education provision. It's great when kids attend the local nursery school and have a chance to make friends in the neighborhood, but unless you are intending to stay in the host country "forever," consider when you will transfer your child to a school that is compatible with your long-term education goals.

Level Six kids are Third Culture Kids[3], but they may have one (of their parent's) culture more dominant than the other. Not every family joins two cultures together in a marriage that enables a third culture to form, but at Level Six the children are quite aware of the cultural differences of their parents. Long-term Level Six living is often for two passport families, where you are choosing to live in one of the parent's countries while raising children. When older, your children will know how to independently go back and forth to "grandma's house," and they forever feel ever so slightly out of place in both cultures.[4]

Level Six Community: If you choose to live at this level, your total focus is on getting to know your host country and you are not interested in being part of the international community. You will want to live in a neighborhood where you are the only foreign family (almost impossible in many major cities), and join host country dominated social groups. You do go home, or to the country of the other passport holder in your family for special events, but choose to also go on vacations where your other host country friends take their families. You learn the host country language or dialect.

Type A Level Six Community (City Level Six)

Try as you might, if you choose to live in a major international city, it is going to be difficult to find, never mind be friends with true host country people. They have seen it all before and often know how to spot a foreigner a mile away. They may avoid you. You may want to know them, but it is rare for them to want to put the energy into someone who they imagine will leave after a year or two. They may be recovering from this type of experience with someone of your nationality. Even host country schools would prefer to not have your children if you are only there for a specific period of time. They want to know how committed you are to their part of the city before forming friendships or sometimes even accepting your children into the local school.

I know several families who have said that all they can hear around them are the accents of foreigners (not of the host country), and they find very little evidence of host country people living near them or eating out in the local restaurants. You may have your child in a local English school for example, but the first question you are asked by other parents at the school gate is, "How long are you going to be here?" City Six families may indeed try to live as a native of the host country, but in an international community, it will be a real challenge. You may choose a host country school and curriculum, select a neighborhood that has the best chance of having host country people, and attend host country social groups, and still feel as if you are spending all your time with people from quite a variety of countries.

In London, your children could attend an English school, your family may be living in south London and attending a Church of England church, and still you find yourself knowing not more than one or two people who carry an English passport or live according to traditional English culture. Many *English* people living in London would do well with their busy schedules to gasp down a cup of tea at the traditional tea time these days. They, too, might be longing to head to the countryside to see something of England. Don't get me wrong, there are pockets of English city life alive and well in a variety of London communities, but you won't see them for at least the first year.

Type B Level Six Community (Countryside Six)

This level is for people who prefer small city, town, or even rural living. Everything around you will be according to host country ways and means. You will be the token foreigner; and if you are living in England, for example, people who never venture up to/down to London may surround you. It's like Connecticut people who just never make it down to Manhattan to see a show. It isn't necessarily a slower way of life in the countryside or small town, but it is often more defined by the host country ways of doing things than in the larger international capitals of the world. Living on this level means that you have accepted that the onus is on you to adjust to host country life.

Dinner Party Test: You mostly invite host country nationality friends and family to dinner. You learn to cook and serve your meals according to host county ways and means. You know people will make allowances for you being foreign, but you do your best to adjust. You ignore what everyone says about your country of origin. You are out numbered.

Level Seven

In Level Seven you will find people who prefer to bury themselves so much into their new culture that they do not go home even for their mother's funeral. One of our local librarians is a Level Seven. Her accent had changed so much that I had no idea she was American until she confessed this to me one day. She swore me to secrecy. She wasn't a spy. She wasn't a criminal. She was just someone who preferred the English culture and had no wish to go home.

The Family: Families who choose a Level Seven Relocation leave their home culture and totally take on a new culture. This is an extreme choice, yet there are people who have gone so far into another culture they do not know the way home. Some people may have had difficult childhoods and this is a fresh start, a new beginning.

Children of parents who prefer a Level Seven Relocation are predominately One Culture Kids, who may or may not know about their parent's previous life in another country. If they do learn that "mummy was born in America," then out of curiosity they may explore their parent's "other culture," but they rarely take this other culture on as their own, as only one culture has been taught at home.

Level Seven Schools: You prefer to send your children to a school where most of the other pupils are from the host country and the host country curriculum is taught in this school. Long-term education goals for your children, should this be appropriate, are only for host country choices.

Level Seven Community: You choose to live in a community dominated by the host culture. You purchase your food items from nearby host country stores and rarely have items sent from your home countries—though you may accept a package or two from your mother if you are speaking to her.

Level Seven Social Support: You choose your social support networks mostly made up of the host culture nationality. You join churches, clubs, and social activities that do not normally include your nationality of origin. These social networks consist of people from your host country culture. You may even decide to change your legal nationality so that you take on the political as well as social responsibilities of this host country. As there is often a sense of loss, when selecting this level of relocation, it is important that you attend a church that understands emotional healing.

Dinner Party Test: No one knows (other than your spouse) you have any nationality other than the host country nationality and there is no acknowledgment of your country of origin around the table, in food, table setting, or in conversation. Most of your friends are from your host country, and you do not even think about looking up the folks back home.

PREFERENCE REALITY

After I gave a talk on the Seven Levels of moving to the PTA of an international school in London, the headmaster said that he had a parent or two who thought they ideally wanted their children in an international school, but he thought they would have been considerably happier (he certainly would have been!) if they had selected their own national culture school. He was tired of hearing them say, "Well, in American we…" Or, "In Germany we…" He readily agreed that people said this sort of thing from time to time, but in a Level Three to Five School (an International School using the International Baccalaureate curriculum), most people just contribute ideas from home, not demand that things be done their way. These parents were out to change the school!

Sometimes we *like the idea* of relocating at one level, but the reality is that we might be more suited to another level. "I need to be with my people" said Marlene, my friend mentioned earlier. She was half joking. She wasn't particularly looking for other Jewish people as she had finally found a lovely synagogue, but finding friends turned out to be the reason for relocating to midtown Manhattan instead of sticking it out in Connecticut. As her children were now grown, a desire to relocate wasn't about walking her kids to school (instead of loading them on the school bus), or worrying about driving in snow; she simply wanted to meet some like-minded people for coffee!

CORE VALUES

Take a moment to consider whether or not it could be easier for you to fit into another culture that has a different language but shares some of your values. For example, you may not speak Italian, but if you share the value of *welcoming* children to restaurants or believe elderly people or religiously garbed people have a right to go to the head of any line, or that lunch should be savored, you may be quite happy living in a small Italian village at Level Six, even if you only have Level One Experience in overseas living. You may find that sharing this view of life enables you to live happily in Italy, even more than in a country where you understand and speak some of the language but totally disagree about how to raise your children.

ADAPTABILITY

Sometimes God closes a few doors and makes it clear that He has a Level in mind for us, one we might not normally choose for ourselves. A client of mine whom I will call Caroline, was a "reluctant Level Three." She had hoped to have the option of sending her children to an American School and live in a fairly American neighborhood, just to minimize the impact of the relocation on her family. However, on her first day visiting London on her research trip, she realized she was more of a country person than she thought. She liked to live near cities and shop there on occasion, but preferred to live out of the city where her kids could have a large backyard and the neighborhood was full of bicycles and BBQs.

There are five American schools in the London area and four of the five schools are outside the city. The four schools, however, were not all-American but had quite an international student population. Three of the schools had changed their names from The American School in Egham or Hillingdon or Cobham, to the International Community Schools. Caroline decided that as the schools offered the American curriculum alongside the international curriculum, and American kids were at least for the moment the largest of the student groups attending the schools, she would place her children in one of these schools.

When the day came for the kids to start school, Caroline gravitated toward the other American families and was happy to see that the teachers spoke to the children with the respect and affirmation that reminded her of home. Even the first grade reading stickers were from an American Parent-Teacher Store. Though Caroline was living in a small English town and had to learn how to use the currency, drive on the other side of the road, and shop in local stores that did not offer some of the things her family was used to having for dinner, she managed to keep her life as American as possible. From a distance, she watched the mothers from a variety of countries who also had children in the same class as her children, but as she had never lived overseas before, she had no idea how to approach them.

Through morning coffees offered at the school, she gradually made a friend from Bergen, Norway. Caroline learned that this Norwegian mom was quite lonely, and though she spoke English quite well, she wanted to meet new people. They became good friends and eventually even started a small Bible study together, which resulted in an invitation for Caroline and her family to have an unexpected holiday to the Nordic countries—with her new friend as the tour guide. You just never know!

WITHIN YOUR HOME

In the part of Surrey where I live there is only one other American living in the next village. Both of our husbands are English (well, he is Italian-English and my husband is English-English), and her husband jokes that we should start our own American Women's club—just the two of us. We have said that if ever a Starbucks comes our way we will do just that!

Being married to an Englishman, *and* with two children born in England, *and* the rural nature of where we live, I would normally have no choice but to live a Level Six, Type B Countryside lifestyle. While this is a beautiful part of the world, I find I can never agree enough with *any* culture to *always* want to be the one who has to fit in. I love our home and our life together, but we have made it our very own and much preferred, Level Four.

To make this a Level Four Relocation (having moved from London two years ago), I used my research trip(s) to seek out anyone and everyone in the area from overseas, to enjoy along with my new English friends.

Part of my decision to move to this area was that there is an international Christian training center, called Pierrepont[5] nearby and a small international church in that same village.

We have Level Four dinner parties on a regular basis, and I am thankful that we live not too far from London. Quite a few of our English neighbors are "London Transfers" and several are foreigners like me. This is where I want to live and when not traveling to visit family in Europe or North America, we bring the world to us as much as possible.

You cannot live every relocation level in every location, but you can take aspects of each level and form your own that works for you. Knowing your preferred relocation level can help you plan of one of the most vital keys to a successful overseas relocation—your research trip.

Level Questionnaire

Take the Relocation Level Questionnaire found at Appendix B and see which level might be right for you at this time. This is a questionnaire for parents, not for children. Remember, though, it's important to include your teenagers and listen to their preferences. There are no right or wrong answers in this questionnaire. God has given you responsibility for your family life and you need to know the desires of your heart. Take a moment to be honest with yourself.

In the next chapter we look at how to take your relocation preferences and plan a successful research trip for your family. You will see how knowing your Relocation Level can help you find a new school, house, community, and social support all in one week!

Chapter Three

CHECKING OUT
THE GIANTS

―――◆◆◆◆◆―――

THE RESEARCH TRIP

Some people are astonished to know that within one week they can find a school, neighborhood, home, a short list of places of worship—and a route to work. Others find it overwhelming to even consider taking time away from their desk to look at a school or house. But if you are going to relocate your family, you need to plan a research trip; and for at least one week, you need to give the trip your focus. While you may want to bring your Blackberry or iPhone to stay connected with the office, tell them that during your research trip your family is the first priority over whatever happens at work. You need to take care of home if you want to take care of business.

In this chapter you, as parents, will see how to organize a one-week research trip that will enable you to select schools, a home, and begin to establish a family support network.

The first key to a successful research trip is to remember that you are on a trip to check out the giants. The giants can be tricky. If you don't know your giants, you can spend a lot of time sorting them out after your move. The giants will do their best to ensure you spend more time putting out family bush fires than accomplishing anything at work. The giants will target your time, money, peace, and joy. The giants want to send you packing and cause your relocation to fail.

But the fact that there are giants in your new location does not mean that you forget about relocating. If God has said to go, the giants are for information only. A typical relocation giant, for example, might be school placement for your children. It may be that at the time of the year you need to move, spaces may not be available in the schools you choose. Your refrain needs to be, "Whenever things seem impossible, the Lord's arm is not too short!" (see Gen. 18:14; Isa. 50:2, 59:1; Jer. 32:17,27) or "Nothing is impossible for God."

If God has given you the word to go, He will display His power to confirm His word (see Gen. 18:14). The best thing you can do is trust God in every detail and not waste time grumbling about your move (see Num. 14:27). In Numbers 13, the Lord commanded Moses to check out the land. He wasn't sending people to collect information that would determine if they should or should not relocate, but to see what they would be up against when they moved, to see what the people who lived there were like, and "what kind of towns do they live in?" (Num. 13:19).

The second key to a successful research trip is an attitude of gratitude. We need to have a "different spirit" (Num. 14:24) that looks at what the Lord is going to do for us as we move into where He has called us to live. This is why it is so important in our relocation strategy that our first step mentioned in Chapter 1 is to know that He has both told us to go and that He promises He will go with us.

Moses did not want to even think about relocating without God. "If Your presence does not go with us, do not send us up from here" (Exod. 33:15). Thankfully the Lord agreed, saying, "My Presence will go with you and I will give you rest" (Exod. 33:14).

So What Are the Giants?

The giants are anything that you are unsure of and you know you *need* to sort out so that you can focus on the job at hand.

You *need* to know that your children are happy at school. You *need* to know that your family has a good place to live, and you *need* to know that there is a network of support for your family life. Whether you are planning a home country relocation or an international relocation, this chapter sets out how to have an organized and stress free as possible research trip.

Giant Number One: Schools

Your first giant is schools. It is easier to find a place to live near the school you want, than to find a school near the home you want. I recommend you look at schools for your children before you finalize a place to live. Many parents feel they could be happy living in a house that wasn't perfect, if their kids were happy at school. Some parents have a desire to choose their church or synagogue before they do anything else, and I will address that in a moment.

Please remember it may take awhile to get familiar with the different terminology used for the various school systems. Public schools are private (in England), and private schools are more often than not referred to as *independent*. In the UK, the term *public school* refers to very specific selective, private schools, such as Eton, Harrow, or Winchester.

As a rule, American schools that are open to all local residents are called *public*, and schools that charge a fee for students to attend are private. In most other parts of the world, non-fee paying schools are referred to as *state schools*, and fee-paying schools are *independent*. For more information regarding the state and independent UK schools, visit www.direct.gov.uk. Most European International Schools are fee-paying independent schools.

When you schedule school visits, focus on the schools in your preferred relocation level.

Level 1 and 2 schools: Your own nationality schools

Level 3, 4, and 5 schools: International schools

Level 6 and 7 schools: Host country schools

In Chapter 4, I will get you started on drawing up your list of schools to visit, but for now let me say that you will need to *make all school appointments before you get board the plane.* Focus on making appointments from your preferred level school list and then, if there is time and availability, add one school from each of the other relocation categories. For example, if you are interested in only your own nationality schools, visit those schools; then add one international school and one host country school to your school visit schedule. A year from now you will want to know that you checked out the possible school categories before making your final decision.

Six Schools

I suggest you visit a maximum of six schools on your research trip. If you work on making school contacts before you leave home, you should be visiting only your short list of schools. We have found that six schools gives you plenty to compare, and not too many to send you into "information overload."

Try to visit only three schools per day. Years of experience has taught that you need to avoid the temptation of squeezing in a fourth school on any school visit schedule. Headmistresses and principals who have led tours of their schools to busy corporate executives can tell when you have simply added their school to your list of places to see and haven't done your homework. If you keep to "three schools a day," you will have a more relaxed pace and can take a minute to look in a classroom or listen to a child learning to read. Later in this chapter you will see a schedule that has successfully worked for nearly a thousand parents.

Giant Number Two: Neighborhood and Home

Picking a house is more than just checking out the number of bedrooms. Do not be tempted to tell your realtor to "just give me something with three!" You need to seriously consider the surrounding neighborhood. Do you like hills? Do you have a choice? Are you happy with an apartment if you know that a park is nearby? Is your potential home fairly maintenance free, or are you going to be spending a lot of time fixing things, such as the plumbing, if they fail to work? Will you have enough storage? Should you bring your furniture? (usually, no).

Not every country has multiple listings for rental homes, so this is where a relocation agent is very helpful, indeed. Debbie Grant, who has served the London community for many years, says that various nationalities have markedly different requirements when it comes to renting or purchasing a home. "Americans like storage space! Germans often want to come with their quite large furniture," and she could go on with a list of what national groupings want for their families. This is not stereotyping. This is recognizing that some cultures desire different layouts when it comes to home design, and this impacts family life. A good relocation agent knows her city or town and will do her or his best to locate what you need. A good relocation agent also knows the questions you need to ask, and will prepare a short list of accommodations for you to visit. What would take years for you to sort out, professionals like Debbie sort out in a week.

If a relocation agent is not part of your relocation package, then know that many international schools have someone who can assist you with finding accommodation, or at least find a reliable realtor/estate agent. Whatever you do, speak with someone who knows and lives in the community before you board the plane for your research trip. You need to identify the family-friendly areas of town before you set your heart on a house or apartment.

Giant Number Three: Social Network

For faith-based families, this is your church or synagogue. You need to decide whether or not you are happy to drive to a place of worship, or what public transportation is available. If you have a list of churches, take time to telephone the offices and see where you find a warm welcome. Again, if possible, do this before you leave home.

Gay Mallam, who ran our Childtrack office in the UK, checked out an entire New Jersey town's church offices (with her British accent), just to "test the welcome." Though this will not check every detail of whether or not this church is for you, it is part of God's plan that His church welcomes people, as well as teaches them, and heals those who need healing (see Luke 9:11). By the way, though the town needs to remain anonymous, it was a black Pentecostal church that was the "Warm Welcome Winner."

Ask your pastor or priest or rabbi for a recommendation of churches or synagogues in your new location. See Chapter 3 Endnote 1 for a church locator Website. If you start your research trip on a Saturday and leave the following Sunday, you will have a chance to visit two churches.

Just remember that while finding potential churches or synagogues can be a challenge, your *faith family* is not a giant. Your new church family is a gift from God. You will do your part on this research trip by looking at options for schools, housing, and a new church; but you need to trust that if He is sending you, He knows exactly where He wants your family to worship.

Families that are planting new churches often hope to find a school in the new community as a way of helping with their social networking; but for this research trip, focus on looking at all your options and check that you are not insisting that your child attend a school simply to give you more credibility with the community.

YOUR RELOCATION TEAM

You need a knowledgeable relocation team that will be available to speak with you in the days leading up to your research trip. Your team will make appointments for you to visit schools, drive you around, give you information on neighborhoods, and inspect houses with you.

Check that your relocation team lives where you are relocating. I am still surprised at just how many people hire relocation teams that do not actually live in the new location. One company serving New York City has used an education consultant who lives out West. To me, that may be the definition of crazy thinking. Your human resource staff member can live anywhere as he or she works as a coordinator for your relocation team, but they need to work with a realtor/estate agent and education consultant who actually lives in the new location.

You may not be in a position to hire a relocation team, or your organization may not be in a financial position to provide a ready-made team for you, but you still need the team. Missionary organizations and NGOs often have someone who is already on-site to show you around and answer any questions. If possible, ask them to make both housing and school appointments for you or give you the contact details so that you can make those appointments before you leave home.

You need four people on your Relocation Team:

1. The Relocation Team Coordinator: Everyone reports to this person. The Coordinator enables the education consultant and the estate agent to work together and pulls together your schedule for your trip. He or she will report to your HR Department and work as the information hub for all concerned with your move. If you are your own coordinator, make multiple copies of your school visit schedule (copy the sample schedule found at Appendix C) so that you and your spouse have your own copies, and leave a copy back home with whoever is looking after the kids. If the kids are with you, or you have teenagers who need to visit the schools themselves, then make additional copies. This schedule is invaluable as a memory jogger when you get home and say "remember that second school we saw, with the attractive

classrooms?" and some family member says, "no that was the fourth school we saw"…you get the picture.

2. Your Driver: While many professional drivers can get business people from the office to the bar/pub, you need a professional driver who knows where the schools and family restaurants are located. Do not compromise on this member of the team. He or she will save you valuable time and can advise you on excellent routes to school and office, and might even give you the latest update on the best car to drive for that city. You cannot be late arriving for school appointments, and it is false economy to try to get around on public transport in most cities only to miss the school you are most interested in for your children. Disregard this statement if you are moving to Amsterdam. (Enjoy the smooth interconnectedness of train and bus!)

3. The Education Consultant: This person will have confidential information concerning your education requirements, though he or she will be responsible for ensuring that your schools are fully aware of any and all special needs. This information may not be shared with the estate agent unless you give him or her permission to do so. The Education Consultant helps you to choose schools for your children, and will coordinate with the real estate agent so they know where to start the house hunt. Education consultants suggest that you never sign on the dotted line for a house until you have it in writing that you have been accepted for a school. If, due to budget concerns, you are the education consultant, try to find a school counselor who has had recent relocation experience. You need someone to "bounce ideas" with and discuss pros and cons. Check that your consultant will be contactable and available to talk during your research trip. Again, in international schools you will find teachers who have had transition experience. These teachers are supportive of families on the move, and can often advise when a child needs special assistance with learning challenges, or just few months to settle in.

4. The Estate Agent/Realtor: Accommodation should support education. There are fabulous realtors in this business. They

are the ones who will not push you into signing for a house until you know where your children will be attending school. They are professional about not giving school advice and will work closely with the education consultant to support the family decision regarding school selection. Some realtors assist with making school appointments, but take great care if they start telling you that they know a "wonderful school," or show concern that some nationalities are "behind" and would find the local school curriculum challenging. A school that has experience with academic cross cultural transition doesn't always advertise itself and the little village school may just surprise you. If you do not have an education consultant to advise you about these rare gems, then do your homework and speak to a member of the academic staff or the head-mistress of any school you are considering.

In Chapter 4 there is additional information on what to check out when visiting a school.

PREPARATION FOR YOUR RESEARCH TRIP

Like interior decorating, a successful research trip comes down to prep work. Often you have only three weeks' preparation time for making this trip, and having this sort of time frame can do wonders for your focus. During this time, you need to have several chats with your education consultant and your housing consultant so that they have an idea of your requirements.

Based on the type of schools your children need, the education consultant and the housing consultant will begin the process of narrowing down areas and communities that suit your family. These two consultants need to work closely together to prepare for your visit. Often the education consultant can make the housing consultant's job easier by narrowing down school districts.

As mentioned earlier, experience has taught that you cannot take in more than three school visits per day. If you have done the prep work with your education consultant, you should only be seeing your agreed short list of schools while on your research trip.

If you are preparing your own School Visit Schedule (see Appendix C), remember these schools should be at least theoretically suitable for your family and verbally confirm *before your visit* that they *potentially* have spaces for your children. This *does not* mean that a school is offering your children enrollment at the school and you should never pressurize a school to accept your child "sight unseen." Ask the school staff if they need to interview your children, or if school reports and teacher recommendations are sufficient to make a decision of acceptance after your visit.

WHO SHOULD COME WITH YOU?

Bring your teenagers! While it is not appropriate to schlep very young children from school to school and then house to house, you need to include your older children during this week of research.

If you have a child with special needs whom you think should not be left behind with a close relative for the week, then make arrangements before you leave home for a special needs nanny or an additional trusted friend or family member to accompany you.

Most top nanny agencies have several qualified nannies who will come to your hotel, but you do have to book them in advance. We have had a special needs nanny travel with parents as they visited schools, but children are often happier if you can trust the nanny or an energetic relative to take them to fun sights or playgrounds. It is difficult for any child staying in a hotel with adults to suddenly see a classroom full of children and toys and only be able to look! Remember to ask, and not assume, if it is OK for your child to have time on playground equipment in the schools you visit.

NOT A VACATION

While it is tempting to do a little sightseeing or at least some shopping to take things back to the kids, keep these distractions to the barest minimum. If you plan to go away for a week as parents on your own, it is *so* tempting to have dinner with new colleagues or even a friend or relative who "just happens to live" in this new location. That is a great way to relax at the end of a hectic day, but I must take a moment here to say please guard your time and choices wisely. After a busy day of school visits, it is understandable that you may want to discuss your research with your friends; but if possible, do not discuss schools in a way that might pressure you into last-minute schedule changes. If you want to check with a boss or colleagues about recommended schools, do this as part of your *preparation* for your research trip—not while you are on the trip. If colleagues suggest schools that interest you, talk them over with your education consultant or school counselor before you board the plane.

There may be a reason why this school might not be appropriate for your children, and your consultant can help you be diplomatic about this rather than spending the week visiting the schools of every employee's child in your department. Trust your education consultant, if you have one, and make a firm decision about who you are going to listen to or take advice from, as there will be many people who have a vested (and not disclosed) interest in telling you about "the perfect school."

After listening to the concerns of one family about their move to New York from London, we recommended several schools that seemed to be a perfect match for the family. The dad, however, had consulted his colleagues and they all—every single one of them in the department—lived in an area we had not recommended for various reasons. With the needs of both his wife and one of his two children in mind, we discussed our concerns, yet he insisted that we find schools in the area where his colleagues lived. We were open with each other and said that while we disagreed with his decision, we would do exactly as he asked. The family moved to the new area and it wasn't long before we got a call. The dad graciously said, "You've earned the right to say 'I told you so!'"

Have an open debate with your consultants, knowing they very much want to get the right schools and housing for your family.

What to Take With You

Children's school records and samples of work. Standardized testing results have some, but limited, value as another country's educators will be unfamiliar with your standard. However, samples of work and drawings done by young children give a potential new teacher an idea of what your child can and cannot do. Teacher comments on report cards are helpful, too.

Please make a note of the grade your child *will be* in when you anticipate he or she starts school in the new location. Many schools have different cut-off dates for the age your child must reach to be part of a particular grade—or "year group" as it is referred to in England. Remember to check that your child is being considered for the appropriate age match!

Photos of your children. Try to have informal photos of your children, as these often give some idea of a child's personality. One school, which I have promised shall remain nameless as it is one of the very academically top New York City schools, accepted one of our clients as much on the fun photo of dad wearing his daughter's tiara at her birthday as on her academic record. Have at least one photo of your family simply "being family."

Sensible shoes: You will be walking up and down school stairs and through potential houses and neighborhoods.

Smart but casual clothes: You do not need to dress to impress potential headmistresses or principals as they have seen it all. Everyone will know you are on a research trip and not visiting to see the sights. Dress comfortably, but with respect for the fact that you will be interviewing potential school staff.

Familiarize yourself on using the Strengths and Weaknesses Chart in Appendix D. This chart is for you to use to take notes on each school you visit, though you could possibly use it for any house visit as well. In the next chapter you will see how to assess schools on visits and to use the chart to help you both collect information and to make a decision on school selection.

Suggested Schedule for a One Week Research Trip

Following is a suggested schedule for parents on a one-week research trip.

Saturday or Sunday

Fly to your new location and give yourself a little time for your body clock to adjust. By Sunday night you will have had time to visit at least one church service and made contact with both your education and housing consultant. Confirm who is collecting you first thing Monday morning, what time, and where you will meet. Print an updated schedule for the week ahead. It helps to stay in a hotel that has at least a basic business center.

Monday

Have the driver pick you up at your hotel and take time touring your possible neighborhood locations.

Your mind may be focusing on schools and what the neighborhood looks like, but take a moment to consider what you would do should you or one of your children, God forbid, has a medical emergency in that area. Look up addresses of health care providers for your family. Are they conveniently located? Is there parking? If your previous doctor has recommended a new doctor for your family, take a moment to call that person to confirm that you look forward to possibly meeting in the near future. Ask your relocation professional for emergency contact details, and write essential information in both your personal notes and on your school visiting schedule.

No one wants to have a medical emergency; but if you do have a health concern, planning ahead is wise. This example isn't in the heart attack league, but we once had a situation when a young visiting mother had her finger bitten by a classroom hamster in The American School of London. With contacts written in her schedule, we made a quick call to the National Health Service advice number "just to be sure" regarding tetanus shots.

In many European countries, you may be eligible to join the local community medical center. As you tour your possible neighborhoods, make notes of the health care centers and the local hospital. Ask your relocation agent, or a member of your organization's personnel team to guide you in the process of getting good medical care and advice.

With your housing consultant, visit three or four sample houses or apartments. The purpose is not to find the house of your dreams, but to familiarize yourself with what's available. So when you find the school you want for your children, you can say, "Remember that house I saw on Monday that had the three bedrooms and was across from a park? Can you find something like that but in the _____ school area?"

If you have never visited the country before (and even if you have visited as a tourist), you need an idea of what is available, so your housing person can swiftly adjust your accommodation preference after you have selected your school.

Unless a school has full-time admissions staff, try not to visit classrooms on Mondays. Teachers worldwide are trying to settle in their students and start new topics at the beginning of the week. They do not need parents traipsing around classrooms and taking teachers away from their pupils. Of course, most of the larger international schools have full-time admissions people, whose sole job is to give you a school tour and process your application form. Admissions staff know which classrooms to "pop into" (Monday's included) and which rooms need to be quietly tiptoed around as an exam might be in process. Still, I prefer to schedule school visits on Tuesday and Wednesday, as that leaves time for house hunting or scheduling additional school visits, should that be necessary.

Tuesday

8:00 A.M.	Your education consultant meets you at your hotel for coffee and a school visit chat
9:30 A.M.	First school visit (record your thoughts in the Strengths and Weaknesses Chart)
11:00 A.M.	Second school visit (record your thoughts in the Strengths and Weaknesses Chart)
12:30 P.M.	Lunch (review Strengths and Weaknesses Chart)
1:30 P.M.	Third school visit (record your thoughts in the Strengths and Weaknesses Chart)
3:00 P.M.	Return to hotel (review Strengths and Weaknesses Chart)

Try to not make a decision regarding schools at this point, as you will not have seen them all yet. Tuesday is often the day when our human bodies "hit the wall" after a long-haul flight, so take the evening off to visit the theater (unless you think you'll waste the money spent by falling asleep), see a film, or rest up with a good book before you start your second round of visits.

For "decision-makers," Tuesday is often the most difficult day of the research trip as you want to select a school and get on with other details. Patience is still a virtue. Friday is the difficult day for "information collectors." They can't get enough of collecting info and wonder what they are missing if they don't see just one more school.

Wednesday

9:30 A.M.	First School Visit (record your thoughts in the Strengths and Weaknesses Chart)
11:00 A.M.	Second School Visit (record your thoughts in the Strengths and Weaknesses Chart)
12:30 P.M.	Lunch (begin filling in school application forms and review Strengths and Weaknesses Chart. Talk with housing consultant about first-choice schools that have potential openings)
1:30 P.M.	Last School Visit (record your thoughts in the Strengths and Weaknesses Chart)
3:00 P.M.	Return to hotel to discuss and select your first, second, and third school choices.

Eliminate other schools from your list. Complete application forms and photocopy all necessary forms. All applications should be hand-delivered by the end of the working day. Make thank you telephone calls to any school that did not make your top three list. Any school place that is not appropriate for you family, will be wanted by another family. It isn't fair to hold a possible place that could go to another child. Liaise with housing consultant to confirm house or apartment visits in your school preference areas.

Thursday

Visit potential houses with your housing consultant. While you are visiting houses, the education consultant should check with schools regarding application processing time frame. Arrange for registration fees to be paid to any independent or private schools, but *do not pay* any deposits or school fees until final school selection and acceptance has been made. You may be liable for a full term's fee if you pay a deposit and for any reason your child does not attend the school.

Friday

Revisit potential houses or school neighborhoods. Most schools will not make appointments for Friday afternoon, but you can make an appointment for the morning and it is always a good idea to stand outside and watch the kids and parents at the end of a long school week. This is your "margin day," and you will need this time to complete any necessary paperwork and confirm decisions made.

Saturday and Sunday

If possible, visit your second church or synagogue.

Spend time in neighborhoods checking out shopping, library, services, and places of interest in your new community; if possible, visit your second choice place of worship.

Fly home.

THE FOLLOWING WEEK

Think about how you feel regarding the school selection. Sometimes when you are back in your normal decision-making territory, you feel differently about choices you've made. If you have any questions, arrange a time to review your choices with your education consultant or school counselor. Just because a school says there are plenty of spaces, does not mean you have a lot of time to accept an offer of placement for your children. Remember there are thousands of kids moving around the world and school spaces go quickly. A verbal offer from an admissions office is not the same thing as a letter of acceptance from the admissions office, which tells you when and how you need to confirm the offer.

You need to write to the school or schools of your choice, at least via e-mail, to accept the offer of placement for your child or children. After you have an acceptance in writing and you have responded in writing, then pay your deposit for school fees and kindly let the other schools know that while you appreciate your chance to visit their school, your children will be attending another school. Thank you notes to headmistresses are always appreciated.

Chapter Four

THE ACE CARD

I don't know what you think about poker. When I was growing up, my deep South, Southern Baptist parents made sure we knew that you just might be going to hell if you played with cards. In some Southern circles you could play Fish or War, but not on Sundays. I suppose it is with a slightly rebellious heart that I wanted to learn how to play poker. It is with a sensible mind, though, that I restrict my stakes to match sticks or pennies in a devalued currency, and it is with a love for my parents that I will not play in their house.

It was while sitting in the basement of The American Church in London that I looked at this Southern heritage and began to understand that I was a third culture adult (or TKA in "relocation speak"). David Pollock (one of the chief professors) and Ruth Van Reken (researcher and writer extraordinaire) were speaking at the church that day. As the ancient English capital of Winchester, where I lived at the time, was fresh out of cross-cultural parenting courses, I was glad these people had made it to London. I was attending their talk, as a parent, to receive some global parenting advice.

"Put your hand up," said David, "if you are a third culture child yourself." Almost no one raised a hand, and David looked bemused. "OK," he said in a fun manner that said he truly had his work cut out for him, "let's talk about how many of you are married to someone who is not your nationality." That would be us, just about all of us in the Fellowship Hall. As David went on to talk about two people from two different countries raising a child in yet a third country, it dawned on me that I, too, might have been a third culture child.

Both of my parents are American, yet one is from a farm in North Carolina, and one from Arkansas/Texas (long story) and they raised me, my brother, and sister in Washington, DC. My parents were country kids making sense of a big city in the 1960s. Two different accents, food, customs, environmental memories (which state had the best peaches!), and just about zero knowledge of how to raise city kids. It might not be two foreign countries, but in some ways I could see how the issue of merging two cultures on a third terrain got me started on cross-cultural living.

While David Pollock was explaining the aspects of merging (merge/takeover?) cultures within a family, I thought back to my first grade classroom. I remembered my teacher announcing the start of National Breakfast week. She said that we would be learning about healthy food. We would also be learning how to read some of the basic food words. My teacher stood at the board with chalk in hand saying, "Now, does anybody want to tell me what they had for breakfast today?"

I was not a terribly shy child, so my hand was the first to shoot up.

"Yes Kathy?" said Mrs. Robinson, my gentle teacher, smiling at me.

My mom had made my favorite in the whole world breakfast for me that morning.

"Grits," I said.

The teacher stood still for a moment. For a fleeting second I was concerned for her. What if she didn't know how to spell it? I sure didn't. But what she said next I will never forget. The entire classroom was having one of those pin-dropping-you-could-have-heard-it moments.

"What are grits?"

The room burst into an uproar. I was mortified, and needless to say, never shared this type of thing with my classmates again. I quickly learned that inside my mother's kitchen it was Carolina South, and on the playground it was Northern territory.

When David and Ruth finished their talk, David smiled and asked again, "Anyone think they just might be a third culture kid themselves?"

I shot my hand up, along with many others who had gained understanding that day.

BACK TO POKER

As parents—third culture or otherwise—we seek to collect good information and make wise decisions. We want to know how to raise our children whatever the terrain. My parents never expected to raise city kids. You may have never expected to be raising children at least some of the time in another region or another country. There can be a temptation to complain to HR about the hand you have been dealt (read relocation package) but whether the chips are up or down, as parents we cannot lose this game. Wherever we move, we cannot gamble with our children's education. The stakes are very high, and the decisions we make affect a generation.

In Chapter 1, you were challenged to make a stand for your personal priorities in life, asking God if He wants you to relocate. In Chapter 2 you examined the level of move you believe you are being called to make. And in Chapter 3 you made plans to organize a research trip to your new location. This chapter focuses on what to look for when you are visiting your short list of schools.

"FLYING" VISITS

Let me say here that you are not a school inspector; and even if that happens to be your day job, it is a challenge to make accurate assessments as you "fly through" potential schools. Even if you are fortunate enough to have a school teacher as an education consultant, you need to check that the consultant only books appointments for you to visit schools that:

1. Have a good reputation in the community.

2. Do not use corporal punishment on children.

3. Have a clear curriculum and communication plan.

You need to know if a school has set policies to take physical and emotional care of your child *and* teaches him or her in a manner that facilitates learning. When I was in teacher training, they used to say, "A teacher sets the environment for learning."

In New York, parents often talk about supposed "A List" or "B List" schools, and by this is meant academic standards, not whether a school is suitable for your child. In London, there are the school league tables. These tables, or lists of schools from recognizable organizations such as the New York

Parent's League (www.parentsleague.com), the London Focus Information Service (www.focus-info.org), Paris's The Message (www.messageparis.com), or the International School Services (www.iss.edu). For China, check out the Newcomers Club directory (www.newcomers.com), which can put you in touch with up-to-date information.

Don't forget the U.S. Department of State, Office of Overseas Schools Website (www.state.gov).

Sites such as these are very good places *to start* your information gathering. Wherever you move, there are Websites to give you initial contact details. Nothing, however, beats knowing the schools themselves; the inside of classrooms, the quirky Wednesday morning whole-school assemblies, the art show, the teacher who loves to take children all the way to the top of Parliament to get close to Big Ben.

And you only get that sort of information by knowing what to look for when you visit! With so much information to collect, let my checklist guide you as you begin to sort out what is and isn't important for you and your family. I call this checklist the ACE card.

So What Is ACE?

ACE stands for Academics, Communication, and Environment. Under each of these headings, I set out the type of information you need to collect and give you a core checklist to review before you begin your visits. Photocopy the checklist at Appendix E and pack it into your pocket as you go from classroom to classroom.

I'd love to say have a practice using this checklist on the school or schools that your children now attend, but if you are the support spouse reading this, the first quiet, sane moment you might have is on the plane.

A is for Academics

There is an old fashioned word: *diligent*. We don't send our children to school to mess around or to be bored. While some parents consider school to be a babysitting service, most of us in the working world expect our children to make considerable academic progress. We know they need to learn diligence—the ability to apply themselves, to focus on developing their identity, and know they have what it takes for a fulfilled life.

While everyone wants their child to be diligent in what they do when they enter a school building, we need to look inside the classroom to see if there is an academic program that will enable them to realize their personal potential. We must know exactly what we mean when we classify a school in the area of academics, and match this with the needs of our child. It's time to be realistic.

To rate a school regarding academics you need to consider three things:

1. Style of academic program.

2. Type of academic program.

3. The amount of push.

Let's look more closely at these three considerations:

1. Style of Academic Program

Most education systems breakdown into three styles: traditional, contemporary, and alternative. All three can be innovative, and you must look for the innovation. In each school you visit, ask yourself "where's the spark?" In every academic program, there should be a spark, something that connects with your child that will pull him in and create a desire to be diligent about learning in that environment (more on assessing the environment below).

Traditional Academic Style

Traditional academics are found in a school that is totally focused on math, science, and first language. Great literature is of paramount importance. Classical composers are celebrated along with strong mathematical skills and periodic tables.

When I visit a traditional academic school (and you can find this in quite a few curricula), I look for the inspiring teacher—the one who can get kids to fall in love with Shakespeare, see the wonder of a math formula, and almost want to live in the science lab. In this academic culture, it is cool to be smart. In a good traditional school, the range of standards can be quite wide, but look for the teachers who look at each child and see something worthy of encouragement. These teachers may not have much time for what they call "soft subjects" or a variety of new teaching methods, but they have all the time in the world for an inquisitive child.

Contemporary Academic Style

This school focuses on what they call the "whole child." The core curriculum covers a wide range of subjects, and the arts, physical and social subjects are just as important as the traditional (classic) maths, science, and English. The contemporary school will keep up-to-date with the latest methods of teaching all subjects and explore different ways in which a child learns. You will often find the more highly trained special needs teachers on staff, and they will assist children with various needs right in that school. The contemporary classroom is an all-inclusive classroom; it offers a learning environment that welcomes the very able child as well as children who face learning challenges. There is usually a speech therapist on staff, as well as what is often called a learning resource staff member, whose responsibility is to look after the special learning needs of the children and support teachers providing for those needs.

Again, look for the spark. Where is the delight in the children? Is there any joy in the teachers and the staff? This isn't school pride, but pride in what the school offers each child. Look at the eyes of the teachers, and everyone in the building. Are they all alive with enthusiasm? The school with contemporary academics is a school where staff and students might not talk much about certificates and awards ceremonies, but they enjoy the journey of life-long learners.

Alternative Academic Style

This style not for the faint hearted. The alternative academic program is for the child who needs a "different drummer" teacher. It is a positive choice for a child who responds well to a particular learning style or program. It is not to be used as a negative choice; that is, it isn't a choice for a child who simply doesn't fit in with the traditional or contemporary academic styles. This is not a "too hard basket," and by that I mean, you are at your wits end in trying to find a successful learning environment for your child and you will try anything. An alternative academic school is one where you have considered the alternatives and found an approach that will enable your child to be successful in reaching their potential.

This may be a school that focuses on visual arts and gives your visual learner a key to successful living and learning. This may be a music specialist school, a ballet school, or one that gives those who struggle with dyslexia the keys to reading. There are schools that focus on the special needs of autism or downs syndrome. These schools offer pupils the keys they need to be all they can be. A life full of ballet or violin or simple communication, but alternative academics also looks at the child and focuses on a personal program for optimum learning excellence.

Again, look for the spark. Are the teachers sharing a love of their subject? A specialist ski-school teacher may be as tough as old boots, but you will see the love in his eyes for the sport. He will not lead you on about your child's ability in heading to the Olympics, but he'll take you on (the whole family) if you've got what it takes. Someone told you that your child would never communicate? Or read at age level? Or understand mathematics? If you want an alternative academic program for your child, find a school that is sparking with a can-do attitude!

2. Type of Academic Program

The type of academic program has to do with the type of curriculum that is best for your child. When visiting schools, you will be looking at various types according to the level you wish to live in your new location.

Levels One and Two will be reviewing home country curricula. Levels Three, Four, and Five will be looking at international curricula. Levels Six and Seven will be reviewing host country curricula.

If you are undecided about the level that is right for your family, take the time to visit two or more types of academic programs. The tricky bit in any curricula is to check how the stages are set out. For example, is there an exam somewhere along the line that opens or closes a door to the next stage of school life? You will want to know what happens in the year leading up to any major exam, and the impact this might have on your child. Remember, a host country school might not want a child from overseas coming into a class that has jelled over the fast few years and is being prepared for a specific exam.

Your own home country school will want to help your child keep on track for exams that would enable your long-term goals, but a host country school has no incentive to do this. If schools are rated on exam results in some sort of league table, the host country school will be checking to see if your child will affect their results in some way. Many headmistresses or principals will tell you it is not fair to your child to bring them into a class that is in the middle of an exam year. Listen to this advice, no matter how wonderful this school would look on your child's CV.

Features and Challenges

When assessing any type of academic program as a parent, look for what I call the Feature and the Challenge. The Feature is what attracts you to this course of study. Is this a Christian school or a school that teaches some religious education? Do you like the clarity of the math program? Is violin taught at an early age?

When you are touring the school, have your guide tell you what the children learn at each grade or year group. At this stage of your research trip, you cannot assess the standards of teaching, only check what is being taught. Teaching assessment often takes school inspectors days in a single school and you only have an hour, but ask to read any inspection reports. Still, you need to get a sense of what is special about a particular school's academic program. You need to stand in the classroom and ask! Your guide (student, teacher, administrator) may tell you, "we are known for our science," or "we continue to win art awards." That may or may not be a feature for you; but while visiting a school; see if there is anything in the curriculum guide that inspires you and you know will inspire your child.

Also note if there is any area of a school's academic program that seems particularly weak. Ask yourself if there is any part of the curriculum that seems to be missing in what you want for your children.

The Challenge will be anything you believe you will need to do to compensate for what is not offered in the school. Many Christian parents want to know if there is at the very least a daily Bible reading or prayer. Even if you want to teach your faith at home and have your children attend a secular school, every parent has some idea as to what constitutes an important feature of any curriculum. For example, most British parents want to see swimming as part of the primary year's (elementary) curriculum, as it is considered a life skill. Any school not offering this may indeed be a good school, but you might want to ask yourselves, "Can I find a place somewhere near where the children can learn to swim, or is there a school that offers this as part of the Physical Education program?"

So, as you visit each school, ask, "What is the *feature* of the type of academic program provided, and what is the *challenge*."

Special Needs Challenge

There is a saying among parents who have children with special needs that when you have finally secured placement at the school you want with the great speech therapist, etc., then your spouse will come home and announce, "My boss wants to move us to London!"

When you are visiting schools, the *features* will be the therapies offered within the school itself, and the challenges can be the therapies you will need to find outside of school hours.

Parents of children with special needs are often tempted to opt out of overseas assignments, but you may be pleasantly surprised and even find yourself wanting to stay in your host country a very long time indeed.

There are *five things* you must do as you start your school and services shopping.

First of all, you must recognize that even if you are committed to the state/public sector education in your home country, you will need to opt for private schools to get a specialist curriculum in many countries. By the time you work your way through the local government bureaucracy to get the assessments you need (one more time!) for a public (state) school, it would be time for you to go home.

Second, you need to know your own (not just your child's) communication style when it comes to receiving updates on your child's progress. Be ready to accept that reporting styles are different in each country (more on this in following Communication section), and that you may need certain reports for your transition at the end of your assignment. If the host country system won't work for you, take time to agree to an approach with the new school or service provider.

Third, whether your child is in a gifted program or has a developmental delay, you will need to take a translation of your child's assessment, sample of his or her work, and reports of any early intervention program for the youngest children with you to each school you visit. Try to have a statement of what your child can and cannot do, not just a disability label.

Fourth, accept that your child may need to have yet another assessment. In the private sector this will take days instead of weeks and it will be worth it. This can be a sticking point for many parents who feel their children have had enough assessments for one lifetime. Some service providers will agree to a consultation if you have a recent assessment report, if you ask. Others will only trust their own assessments. Instead of this being a negative, try to use this assessment as a way of enabling your child to learn about the new school, and let this be part of your own assessment as to whether or not this school is for you and your family.

Fifth, use national support bodies and help lines as a starting point for locating schools and services, especially if your HR manager has little knowledge of local special needs provision. For example, www.autismintervention.com will give you useful contacts for parents relocating to the UK and Europe and link you to sites for Africa, the Middle East, Asia, South America, and the Caribbean. Though some of these particular links need translators, you can often find someone from the Newcomers Group (see Website address in previous "Flying" Visits section) who will help you with the translation and connect with you the support you need.

3. The Amount of Push

Whether you are observing a traditional, contemporary, alternative academic style or a home, international, host country, special needs academic curricula, it is wise to check just how much push there is in the school. Pushing a child means both the level of expectation teachers have for a child and the amount of time a child is expected to devote to academics in a day.

Check to see if a school knows when and where to push a child to greater diligence with homework, or going the extra mile in exploring her science topic. How do they know if a child needs a little more drawing out in classroom discussions or needs a quiet moment during the day? Do they use encouraging words or ridicule to get a kid going? Star charts on the walls? In other words, how will this school motivate your child to work?

How many hours is your child expected to toil away at homework? When homework is assigned, are parents expected to help or does the teacher want to see what your child can do on his own?

One fifth grade teacher in Connecticut received a note from a parent at the end of the year, thanking him for "keeping their family together, night after night, as we all sat around the dinner table figuring out the new math."

When our kids were young we liked to ski on the weekends. I was very happy to supervise homework during the week, but not too happy to have their time taken away from family adventures on the weekends. Notice how much homework is pushed in any prospective school. If this is a school that requires an 8-year-old to do an hour's homework every night, be ready, or don't put your child under this kind of pressure. Push equals pressure, and you need to know what kind of pressure your child will be under to perform academically in any school you select.

If a school has a teacher who understands academic transition—the challenges a child faces as they move from one academic program to another—they will be able to help you gauge the right amount of motivation needed to help a child make a good start. Ask if there is a teacher on staff who can keep an eye on your child especially in the early days of settling into any new curriculum.

ACE Questions on Academics

1. The academic style at _____ school is:

    ❑ Traditional

    ❑ Contemporary

    ❑ Alternative

2. The academic type of program at _____ school is:

    ❑ Home Country

    ❑ International Baccalaureate

    ❑ Host Country

    ❑ Special Needs (Type _____)

3. For me, the features of this school are: _____
    _____

4. For me, the challenges of this school are: _____
    _____

5. What is the push/pressure level at this school?

    ❑ Just right for my child

    ❑ A little too much/too little but my child could handle it

    ❑ Not appropriate for my child/our family

6. Where is the spark? _____

7. Does the school have a teacher that understands academic transition? _____

C is for Communication

Communication style is a major feature of any learning environment. As a rule, American schools will give you, the parent, regular and detailed information. Each week you will receive some form of communication concerning the progress of your child. Many American schools will e-mail you and answer your e-mailed questions. You will know the school calendar, and even have a copy of it to post on your fridge.

The British system is just about the mirror opposite to the American communication style. You may see your child's teacher for 30 seconds each morning, in the first year or two of school. It is during that time that you can ask "how things are going," but it is not a time for a major teacher conference. More formal parent conferences (on Parent's Night) cover only what can be discussed in five or ten minutes. If you have a particular concern regarding your child, make an appointment to see the teacher one afternoon at the end of the school day. Do not expect an American style telephone call from your teacher, unless there is something seriously wrong.

One British client who was living in New Jersey called me one afternoon. "I nearly passed out," said this upset mother, "Brian's teacher rang me last night and I just didn't know what to say. She said she was calling to tell me that my son did the 'cutest thing' in class! Is she going to do this again?" asked my distraught young mum. To my client, the teacher should leave well enough alone unless her child was misbehaving in class. An American mother would have been delighted with this call. To this British mother, no news is good news.

ACE Questions on Communication

1. What is the communication style of this school?
2. Can you work with this style of communication?
3. How much notice will I get that my child needs me to make a costume for a school play?

E is for Environment

The American School in London (www.asl.org) has wide hallways, and light and airy classrooms stacked with up-to-date resources. American schools are known for their excellent children's libraries, superb playgrounds, and developmentally appropriate early childhood programs.

The Swedish school in London (www.swedishschool.org.uk) is one of the loveliest schools around. There is a very good library for the children, and the candlelight celebration at Christmas is a delight to behold. You feel you are in Sweden the moment you step into this clean, charming school.

The German school in London is stunning (www.dslondon.org.uk). The architecture and the layout of the classrooms is an excellent environment for nurturing children.

In London, as in many major world capitals, we could almost go around the world describing beautiful and nurturing schools for expat kids.

As you visit other countries, you may often be inspired by what they have provided for children and young adults. Years ago I spent a winter term as a student at the University of Moscow. It was a fabulous experience of ballet and opera in surroundings that were themselves works of art. Today's Russian young people tell me about their grand pianos and beautiful marble—and very tough academic standards.

You can't always expect to find beauty in schools, but it is a feature that nurtures a child's spirit. Once you start to notice it, it can become important to you. You start to look for the beauty in each school you visit.

Not too long ago, I flew to Pisa to meet a client couple and their children. When I visited their school, I watched the little girls tiptoe down the gilded stairs in their ballet tutus. This school wasn't expensive. It was just the local little school, but the building was beautiful. The teachers adored the pupils and didn't mind teaching two little American girls to speak Italian. This was a spirit-nurturing school, and my heart sank. How was I going to move them from all this to California? My mind was racing. Stanford area schools? I was about to move them to heavy brown buildings, where in my opinion teachers did not have the resources they needed. Where, at the time, music was optional.

If this family was going back to the states, could I talk them in to moving to North Dallas (www.dallasisd.org and www.pisd.edu and www.friscoisd.com), where the schools are fabulous, the admissions people know about overseas living, and the board of education is serious about assisting families moving back home? I could go on, but you will get the idea that I, like any teacher, like any parent, want beautiful, clean, and healthy environments to nurture our children.

You need to look at the resources in the classroom. Are they clean? Up-to-date? Or are the toys, books, lab materials scruffy and ready for the bin? What about a school uniform? Do you like uniforms? What about a dress code such as the one found at TASIS (a beautiful American-International school near London (www.tasis.com), which has a dress code for the older students and a quite practical tracksuit uniform for the younger ones. Some American schools are full of kids wearing their own idea of what is appropriate to school.

In England they used to say, "the uglier the uniform, the better the education." Thankfully this is not true now, but some uniforms are more attractive than others. One of my clients, who was very happy with her school, said she was sorely tempted to borrow another school uniform for the Christmas photos! Another client had a daughter who insisted that she had to have the "purple uniform school." Thankfully, this is an excellent school for other reasons, but it didn't hurt that she was going to wear her favorite color every day.

Children moving from the Middle East, or other sunny places, to grey European capital cities often delight in seeing classrooms painted in bright colors and with intriguing bulletin board decorations.

Physical and Emotional Safety

The environment isn't just about sunshine and large libraries though, it is also about physical and emotional safety. You need to know if all of the teachers and staff have been investigated through police records regarding child abuse. You need to know that fire drills are held regularly and that the building meets safety standards. In cold winters, are radiators protected so that no child gets burned? In small schools, when was the plumbing last checked? Large schools often have a team of people looking after the maintenance, but in small schools one man may have the responsibility for the entire building.

Is this an emotionally, as well as physically safe place to learn? In other words, can children freely speak their minds in an attitude of respect for classmates and teachers? When teachers talk about a country or culture, do they speak with respect? Can children take learning risks in this classroom?

ACE Questions on Environment:

   1. Does this school's environment nurture my child?

2. Is the staff dedicated to making this school a physically and emotionally safe place for my child to learn?

3. Do we like the uniform? No uniform?

STRENGTHS AND WEAKNESSES CHART

Photocopy the School Strengths and Weaknesses Chart in Appendix D, and use it to record your observations for each school. You cannot carry books around as you travel; yet you can stuff a School Strengths and Weaknesses Chart in a pocket, and use the ACE Card as a memory aid for filling in the chart. This will assist you as you compare schools, checking to see which schools have more features than challenges. By the end of any school-visit day, it is often difficult to remember what you saw in the first school. Have someone, you or another member of your family, make a master chart with notes of everyone's observations in your own shorthand. Make a copy or two of the chart and keep it with you for further discussions on the homeward journey.

Having used this simple system for many years, I continually find it rewarding to see parents learn more about what is important to them and to their children as they do this "flying evaluation" of schools.

Chapter Five

THE HOME SCHOOLING OPTION

———— ◆·◆·◆ ————

There they were, three of the most incredibly beautiful children. With a Somalian mother and an Argentinean father, how could they not be beautiful? Their eyes were full of laughter and curiosity. Their smiles were a little shy at first but broadened into a warm welcome as I was introduced as their home school teacher.

"We are going to have a great time, and the whole of London is going to be your classroom," I said.

Now I had their interest! These three, a girl and two boys, had just arrived in London from Brazil. Their dad was with a major oil company and on a brief assignment at the London office. Both parents had asked me to help these middle schoolers prepare for their next move, to Texas in six weeks time. We would start with a few days of assessments in their grade level for math, English, and science, and then we would hit the museums on Fridays.

In the initial assessment, it became clear that they were grade level or above in the subjects they had studied in their international school in Brazil, but they needed a crash course in social studies. Social studies is uniquely part of the American curriculum, and combines history, geography and government. While the emphasis (whether history or geography or government) often depends on the teacher, I had trained in social studies when I did my high school teaching practice, and I was excited to bring every aspect of this subject alive. We would visit Runnymede and see the origin of the Magna Carta. We would visit the new British Library. We would take in that wonderful London restaurant, The Texas Embassy, as a little "taste teaser" for Texas history. There was so much we could do!

Each Monday I would sit with the children at the dining room table, and we would work on the topics for the week. Their mother supervised their studies Tuesday through Thursday and then, on Fridays we pulled the lessons all together with a visit to a place of interest in the London area. This is one form of Transition Home Schooling; it is a great way to prepare your children when you are "between countries." Transition home schooling is an excellent option for those short-term assignments that last less than a school year.

Transition home schooling has two purposes:

1. *Provides Continuity.* Transition home schooling is a good option for those times when it just doesn't make sense to send kids to a new school for a short period of time. By the time you found the school you wanted, registered them, purchased some appropriate clothes, and the kids even thought about making a friend or two, it would be time to move on. If your place of work has an HR Department, ask for local teacher or tutor contacts to assist you with setting up an appropriate curriculum and then get out and do some research.

   If you do not have this support, ask your children's present teacher if he or she could give you some idea of the work your children would be missing. As Transition Home Schoolers are rarely interested in home schooling for the long term you will mostly likely not want to invest in in-depth curricula. Websites are listed in the chapter Endnote 1 to help you figure out what to teach for a full academic year or short periods of time.

   When developing your home curriculum, take care not to focus too sharply on the details of the curriculum in your proposed new location. It's easy to check out via the Internet which school in which country is teaching various subjects, but you never truly know that your family is moving to that new location until you board the plane. Things happen and overseas assignments are subject to last minute change.

2. *Fills Education Gaps.* One of the major benefits of transition home schooling is giving children time close to "home" (being with the family unit even if it's six weeks in a hotel) where they can take stock of family education goals. Do you have a child who needs a little work in one area of math or reading development? Do you want the family to learn a new language? Have you ever thought of simply writing a family history or putting together a photo album of all your travels and publishing it for the folks back home? Transition home schooling allows you to spend time with your kids and see if there are any education gaps you can fill before the rush of flights, packing, and adjusting to being the new kids in the neighborhood. Transition Home Schooling can be a very precious family time.

Another Reason to Home School

There is a third reason why some parents may choose home schooling, whether for a short period or for the longer term. A representative of Southern Baptist Academy cites the growing opposition to Christian values found in public or state school systems in a number of countries. Should you find that no school in your new location offers the education you want for your children, then now is the time to at least consider the home schooling possibilities. No longer should home schooling isolate you or your children; but instead, it is a way to connect with other like-minded families.

TRADITIONAL HOME SCHOOLING

Victor's dad was with the U.S. Air Force. As a family, they traveled to Germany and then to Spain and then back to Germany and then back to Spain and then when Victor was 8 years old, they moved home to Florida. He knew what it was like to be the "new kid." So years later when Victor and his wife, Laura, moved with their kids to England for missionary training, they looked at the home schooling options.

Laura soon realized that the success of the education of their children depended primarily on each child's learning style. Their son was an auditory learner and the normal classroom most suited his learning requirements. Their daughters, however, were more visual learners and home school was their preferred option.

"I don't want to take credit away from a true traditional home schooler," said Laura. "I had the support of an online curriculum and a teacher at the end of an e-mail who helped me organize it all."

"Traditional home schoolers still do it all themselves. They develop the lessons and correct their kid's work. Sometimes they get together with other parents. For example, if one parent is good at mathematics, then that person teaches your kids and their kids, and then they all go to someone else's home for English class, but each parent is totally responsible for what their child learns. Traditional home schooling is a lot of work for the parent or parents. You set the course for the year and what is to be done each and every day for each and every class."

Books and materials can be expensive and traditional home schooling parents say that even materials purchased on eBay can incur considerable cost. There are Websites for purchasing used home schooling materials and springtime seems to be prime time for the best buys.

There is quite a range of support for the traditional home schooler, including online lesson plans and even whole-course curricula. You will find several Website suggestions at chapter Endnote 2, and www.K12.com is one example of home school support that offers certified teacher assistance, curriculum guides for U.S. public school programs and the international curriculum for kindergarten through twelfth grade.

Sharon Hungerford has traditionally home schooled her two sons through high school. Her family is from North Carolina and they have lived in England and Israel. She suggests that for traditional home schooling, you can purchase one or two online classes so that the kids know how to use the technology, and then get other materials from sales and libraries. "Living in another country and traveling has also been part of our boy's education," said Sharon.

VIRTUAL HOME SCHOOLING

Virtual home schooling is a more recent option. It is technology based and has developed considerably over the past few years. In its embryonic stages you could e-mail a teacher with a question and consider yourself fortunate if you had a response in a day or two. "Now," said Laura, who is home from England and living in Florida but still choosing to home school "I hear back from a teacher in a couple of hours." More than e-mailing, virtual home schooling has developed its course offerings and approach beyond recognition. There are class get-togethers on Web cam and Internet. Communication is via microphone and the students can hear each other and interact. When the teacher is explaining something or introducing a lesson, the pupils can click a button and it sends an electronic "hand raise." The student can press a button with a "frowny face" to show that they do not understand what is being said, or click a button with a "clapping hand," to say they "got it!"

From the outback of Australia where home schools developed using the radio for ranch kids, to the Scola of Sweden, to the gulf coast of Mexico, virtual schools are thriving. Quickly disappearing are the days when a teacher ran into the computer lab on her break from teaching other classes. These days virtual schools are up and running and available as a classroom whenever and wherever you live. The virtual teacher is a real person. He or she may be on the other side of the world, but they set the course outline and content and regularly converse with the pupils on all manner of subjects.

In a virtual school, your child may start with an online program to assess their level of knowledge, and then attend an online class that matches their learning requirements. "There is a world of difference from the early days of distance learning," says Laura, "and I feel very supported as I support my kids being schooled from home."

OLD RED

My grandfather was a school inspector in the outback of the Arkansas Ozark Mountains. In the days before highways or four wheel drive, he would load up the old family horse that he insisted was not a horse but a mule called Red. Red was stubborn enough, but he was also reliable. As granddad ventured across creeks and through brush, he endeavored to keep farm kids well-stocked with good books. He brought education materials to places few teachers ventured to go. Years later I would do the same with an old Peace Corps jeep, delivering books to schools in the hills of Jamaica. There is nothing new in trying to bring education to kids in remote corners of the earth.

In 1905, Virgil Hilllyer convinced a Baltimore bookstore owner to sell a kindergarten curriculum to parents who were unable to send their children to Virgil's school. It wasn't long before Virgil put an ad in *National Geographic*, selling his Calvert School education to parents "near and far." Now the Calvert School serves families in over 50 countries and is recommended by the U.S. Foreign Service.[3]

For hundreds of years educators have worked to serve the children of families on the move. We now face a rapidly changing era of distance learning possibilities; but at the end of the day, as a parent, you will need to select a form of education that consistently works for your family.

Whether Old Red or some new satellite system delivers instructional materials to your door, some things rarely change. You can devote time to researching the best type of education in the world, and have every type of technology and educational gadget available, but study habits and a passion for diligence still need to be instilled. Around the world, kids still have excuses for not getting their homework finished or in on time. A child is a child and good habits need to be taught, whatever form of education you select. Nowadays, the computer can be blamed for not completing assignments. When I was a child, I'm sure our dog was singled out as the culprit. In my Peace Corps teaching, I was usually told by a student or two that "the goat ate the essay." But the excuse that makes me smile is the one from a 1940s missionary cited on the Calvert School Website, "The lions' roaring all night kept us awake."

As you and your family look at the option of schooling your children from home, wherever home may be and for however long you live in that location, may you select a course that encourages your children to be all God meant them to be. May your time together be blessed, and may whatever technology you choose work and always work, and may the lions not roar in the night.

Chapter Six

YOUR SUPPORT TEAM—DO YOU HAVE ONE?

A young couple was standing in the middle of a world famous London hotel. Though surrounded by beauty and glorious antiques, the wife of this couple was, nonetheless, choking back tears. The superb and highly trained hotel staff looked concerned. *Who could cry under the chandelier without everything being set right?* Discreetly, of course.

The couple, whom I will call David and Karen, had just spent an exhausting day with me looking at schools and talking about their children who were back in New York with Grandma. The husband, David, whispered to me that his wife thought she had said something wrong to a headmistress at a school we had visited that afternoon.

As David put his arm around Karen, he looked at me, "She's worried we've blown our chance of being accepted at the school."

David looked again at his wife, who showed no signs of being comforted, and then he motioned to me, "Can you have a word with her?"

"Of course," I said, and led Karen away to somewhere a little more private. I was the couple's education advisor and it was my job to ensure that they had the right schools for their children when they moved from New York to London.

"I am SO angry," Karen nearly shouted when we finally moved down an elegant corridor.

I reeled back slightly, but was comforted by the thought that whatever she had said to the headmistress could be sorted out; the school had liked the family. I also knew Karen's problem was not really about the visit to the school. I truly had compassion for this young mother.

Karen had four children, one was only a couple of months old and one had special needs. Though both the recent birth, and the special needs therapies were challenges, the children were not making this competent mother anxious. It was her husband. And he had no idea.

While her husband had gone through the motions of joining us on the school visits and on the surface looked like a husband fully involved for his family in this move, I sensed he wasn't really with us. He seemed distracted—more focused on starting his new job. He responded well to his Blackberry, but not to his wife's concerns about which school was best for them as a family.

David had spent the day making it clear that he "didn't have the time to get involved" or "overly concerned" about all Karen had to do. While her daily objective would be to enable him to walk out the door each morning and go to work, there was no attitude of gratitude coming from him. She was his support team, but he was not connecting the dots concerning what she needed for job satisfaction. Though most men do seem to "get it" that the support spouse needs support, this guy was in a league all his own.

Inside the bank where he would be working, life would resemble life back at the New York office; in fact, he and his colleagues would sometimes joke that they weren't sure which country they were in. Sure he had unbelievable pressure to be successful with a new project, but the nuts and bolts of his day remained fairly similar to what he could expect from the bank he had known for almost seven years. In addition, he had a brilliant office support team who, according to him, were "ready to anticipate his every need." He intimated that he hoped that someday his wife would reach that standard in caring for his to-do list.

Karen, on the other hand, wanted him to kiss the floor she walked on for agreeing to this corporate assignment, "especially after I have just given birth to a fourth baby!" she cried. She had some considerable adjusting to do in this new country that did not have late night shopping, drove on the other side of the road, and was not in her opinion Europe's most child-friendly nation.

Throughout the day, David had unhelpfully pointed out that they could have been assigned to China instead of England and that at least "they speak English here."

Karen wasn't getting hysterical because of the challenges ahead of living in a foreign city. She was quite happy to learn a new dialect of English (150 new nouns to be learned in the first few days) and she enjoyed the fact that the stores offered a new variety of children's food, and she was ready to rise to the challenge of reinventing her career far away from home.

She was mentally prepared for these changes, but what she wasn't prepared for was the wounding she felt when she recognized how little he cared about what she might need to make things run smoothly at home while he was off working a 70-hour work week. She needed to feel valued by David, and to hear him say it. She needed to be acknowledged as the support team on the home front.

CARING

From my experience, you can always tell when a family is going to be successful on an overseas assignment. The employee and his or her spouse observably care for each other. He wants to make sure she has everything she needs to be content in her new surrounding, and she isn't out to "make him pay" for moving her away from home comforts. Both work to see that each other's needs are met. When this happens, the entire family benefits.

If you have read *The Five Love Languages* by Gary Chapman[1] this is the time to use your spouse's love language. Heading out to a new environment is a great time to practice showing your spouse that you care about your relationship.

SEEKING SUPPORT

Karen, being a mother of four, was under no illusion that she needed help. She thought tears might sign David up to be head of her home team, and while she was at it she would add a few other things. A babysitter would be nice, so she could have a few hours in a grocery store to figure out what was actually on the shelves. In her anger, she added that a driver for the first few weeks of the school run was essential! Oh, and then a doctor who understood American child developmental medical checks and shots and prescriptions for earaches. They had never moved overseas before and Karen keenly felt out of her Level One experience depth, trying to set up a Level Three Relocation. David wasn't sure what was needed to make relocation at any level work for his wife, and seemed to think that saying "you'll be fine" was an answer to everything.

Both Karen and David needed a support team if they were going to successfully settle into their new country. Only pride says you can do it all by yourself and pride wastes an awful lot of time.

I assume that you have read the previous chapters and are firm in the knowledge that:

- Key Number 1 to a successful relocation is that within the bounds of God-given priorities of faith and family, you know that *Father God is directing you or releasing you to relocate to a specific place.*

- Key Number 2 is *knowing the level of relocation* that is best for you and your family.

- Key Number 3 is *you and your spouse are in agreement* about the level of relocation you wish to make for the family.

- Key Number 4 is to plan and carry out a *research trip* in the proposed new location.

You are now ready to organize Key Number 5 to a successful overseas assignment, and that is to *establish a personal support team.* Your relocation team will assist you with the process of moving from one location to another, but it is your personal support team that will nurture what you need to successfully remain in your new location until it is time to move again.

PERSONAL SUPPORT TEAMS

After you have completed your move, the employee needs two teams; the work team and the home team. If you are working for a company that subscribes to core values that match your own nationality and/or faith, there is very little you will need to do to adapt, other than the usual adapting to new situations and the one (hopefully one!) awkward or difficult person that always seems to show up in a work environment.

While it is reassuring to know that you have a good cultural match at work, the challenge is to look at the support you need if you happen to be working in an environment where your own faith or work culture is not the dominate decision maker. If you have joined a company where things are done "the English way," or "the German way" or some other cultural "way," then you will need to find out exactly what that means. If you are part of a religious organization, it can be quite interesting to join another denomination in a tour of duty. My charismatic dentist uncle has a great time each summer with a team of Episcopalian dentists in Honduras. If you have any experience with these two parts of our Christian community, you can just imagine. It's a learning curve. It keeps you humble, but you can certainly use someone on your team who works as a cultural translator to keep things running in unity.

A *cultural translator* is not a language translator. Some cultures that do not share a language do have agreement on "how things are done." This is why you find that some cultures that speak a different language have smoother working relationships than two same-language people who are from the opposite ends of the earth.

Some folks think that more gets done at work over tea breaks, and others think even looking at the water cooler is a waste of time. Some work cultures are adamant about long lunch periods, and others look at the one person who runs down to the deli as a slacker. Find someone you can trust to give you an accurate take on your workplace culture and sign them up for your support team.

I have single friends working in corporate environments who talk of needing "a wife," and they are not talking about getting married. For me when I was single, this might have included a cook (this meant ready-cooked meals when I had no time to cook), a laundry (thank you for all the services in the world where you can drop off the dirty clothes and collect or have delivered at the end of the day!), and a house cleaner (blessings to all who have ever helped with keeping the home front sane).

If you are going on an overseas assignment, the working spouse usually has a "wife." Eighty percent of all overseas assignments are for male employees, though the number of women (with husbands) accepting such assignments is growing. In some countries, this still means the wife organizes staff to help in the home, but be ready for the fact that in most European cities it means you (or whoever is not the employee) might be the home maintenance team. If both of you are working outside the home and are both intending to support each other getting out the door in the morning as well as nurturing the children, then you have a very challenging scenario indeed. I hasten to add that the real world of overseas assignments usually has one person who gets the work visa and one person gets labeled "dependent." IBM labeled me "an appendage" when we went on assignment. Thankfully, I know who I am in Christ.

Most wives who travel with their husbands overseas have their own way of referring to themselves. I prefer the term "support spouse," and it is my firm belief that we make these assignments happen. Well, I would, wouldn't I? (as Robin Pascoe might say!).[2]

The support spouse is the one who makes the assignment successful for the entire family, and has the family rather than the work assignment as the focus. If this is you, you are the one who enables the employee to attend to the work assignment, assists the children in adjusting to schools and community, makes family events happen, and provides an oasis called "home."

Settling the children, training them in cross-cultural transition, and raising them with your family values requires a mother *and* a father. Any relocation, international or across the country, needs someone to focus on the family. It is my suggestion that one of you try to be a full-time at-home parent at least for the first six months of any relocation, and work only part time after that. Someone needs to be home when the children are still living with you, and no one has the love and ability to invest in your children more than you.

Number 1—Home Support Team

If we look back at all of the people or services that Karen, at the beginning of the chapter, wanted on her support team, they would in fact be legitimate types of support if the budget allowed. She needed to get a practical grip on all she had to do to find a new community, school, house, church, or whatever else she thought she needed to raise her family in a strange place.

Instead of screaming at her husband, or even me, she could have been screaming (in the beautiful hotel restroom preferably) at Father God. He can take it. He tells us He is our refuge and He knew before she was born that Karen would be moving to a different country. Karen needed to ask Him, "Father, what do I need here? Help me to speak truth in love to those around me!"

Number 2—Soul Support

Too often when we are building our support team we look at the world's way of nurturing our soul and body. It becomes difficult to distinguish between wants and needs.

For example, there is often a sense of loss when you move from country to country. You can check out a variety of ways to compensate for this loss, including a considerable amount of indulgence.

The difficulty with feeding your soul is that it rarely satisfies for more than a moment. It doesn't last. I could decide that whenever I move to a new country, I need Starbucks! (OK that one seems to be solved these days!) I need my best friend to fly over from Manhattan every month! During January sales day I want my sister!

Unless the spirit is nurtured, you can waste a lot of time trying to feed your soul. How do you nurture your spirit so that your spirit can feed, water, warm, and even heal your soul and body in a strange land? How can you sing in a strange land? And fix the washing machine?

How can you deal with the loss that is felt when you relocate overseas and deal with the practical stuff at the same time? What do you do when you think no one is there for you or even begins to understand what you need to make this relocation work?

The world will give you a list of things to do to nurture yourself. Most of it will feed your soul, but it will not satisfy. It might even develop an addiction or two and you can convince yourself that you will emotionally die if you do not have it, but most things will not give you what you need to live life to the full.

Ask your Creator King what nurtures your spirit. Father God speaks Spirit to spirit. Your spirit is to nurture your soul, and your soul is to nurture your body. If you take on what the world says to do to get what you need, you are going straight to your soul and bypassing your spirit.

With Father God as head of your support team, cheering you on to live out His plans and purpose for your life, and your spouse as number two, let's look at the rest of one suggested line-up!

Number 3: Prayer Partner

Support team member number 3 is your prayer partner. This person is someone called to pray for you concerning the details of your relocation. Sometimes it is someone from your home church prayer group or adult Sunday School class. It is someone who will be in regular contact with you, and you agree to be accountable to that person.

God has blessed me with a husband who is my covering and my rest-of-my-life prayer partner, but I still enjoy having a female prayer partner who will lift up both of us when my husband and I are making major life decisions. I do not reveal anything to her that my husband, Chris, would not approve. It's fun to have a good "girl's chat."

Men need prayer partner support, too. Not every man has the time or inclination to join a men's prayer breakfast or head out on a men's wilderness retreat when they are about to change countries, but I believe it is important for a man to have someone he can pray with man-to-man concerning the direction he is leading his family.

We need older and wiser men and women who know how to live the Christian life in the international arena and who will take the time to pass on their wisdom and knowledge. Find a same-sex Christian who is older and wiser in the faith to connect with, at least via e-mail!

Your prayer partner does not need to be living on the same relocation level that you are at the moment, but they do need to have some knowledge and understanding of the level of relocation you intend to live overseas if they are going to pray for you with some measure of knowledge. The Holy Spirit is quite capable of revealing to them what they need to know to effectively pray for you, but it helps if they have some idea of the challenges you are facing. When you are preparing for your research trip, have your prayer partner pray for divine appointments, and the right school placements for your children, as well as your new place of worship and family accommodation. Have that person pray for you every day you are away on the research trip, and for the decisions you will make after you settle into your new location. This prayer partner is a vital member of your support team.

Number 4: Small Bible Study Group

This is a group you either need to find or start in every place you live. This group will keep you focused on the purpose and plan that God has for your life. You do not need to worry about having a career when you have a team that helps you discover what God has for you to do in your new location. A career will find you!

Your Bible study group will be your family, your brothers and sisters in Christ, and will add value to your life no matter how far you are from home. They may also introduce you to the wider community and provide friendships that last forever.

With your faith as your number one priority, and family number two, this is where friends come in. We are called to live in community, even if it takes a little time to build that community in a new place. Sometimes a large church will offer the variety of support your family needs, but it is in a small group where you make friends.

Number 5: Education Advisor

Families should find schools *first*, and then decide where to live. If you are certain of the level you wish to relocate, use your research trip to visit schools that match that level. If you are uncertain of the relocation level that is best for your family, visit schools that match several levels. There is nothing quite like seeing schools in action to help finalize your decision on how you want to live in your new location.

Even after you have selected your new schools, try to find someone who will be available to discuss any education issues throughout your time overseas. This needn't be a paid consultant. It could be that you find a school counselor who will assist you with focusing on the needs of your children as they go from grade to grade and then on to the next school. Ask this support team member to be your sounding board for any school your children attend overseas. Back home, family members who have never seen the inside of a school in another country may feel that they cannot advise you on how to handle situations that arise, even though you may value the fact that they listen. Find a school teacher with overseas experience to fill this team position.

Number 6: Health Advisor

Eventually your health advisor will be your new doctor and nurse practitioner. Sometimes your previous doctor will be happy to remain your point of reference while you are settling into your new area, but you need to make contact with someone locally who will assist you should there be an emergency.

Contacting a health advisor needs to be a priority while on your research trip, and keep the contact details with you the day the plane lands with you and your children. Ruptured ears happen to little people on airplanes. Even minor health worries need to be sorted out when you want everyone to feel their best for travel or moving into your new home, or for the first day at a new school. Your company HR person or relocation manager can assist you with recommended emergency care numbers.

Number 7: Food Advisor

Having a food advisor may be more of a requirement in countries with a totally different cuisine, but it can be important for families with children who have special dietary needs. It can also depend on the level of relocation you wish to make. If you are hoping to eat as the locals do, or find your home country food locally, then having someone who can tell you how to find ingredients is especially helpful in the early days.

If you are living in a hotel while waiting for your household goods shipment to arrive, make friends with the concierge. He or she should know most food shops and family restaurants that will be useful long after you are living in your own home. Check out some of the recipe Websites at chapter Endnote 3. You do not need to load down your shipment with cookbooks. You can find most recipes online, and even e-mail yourself your favourite recipe notes before you go.

Number 8: Time-Off Advisor

A time-off advisor knows how to find anything that helps you nurture your spirit when you need to rest. This contact may be on the back burner until the boxes are unpacked and everyone is settled in job or schools, but this support team member can be a lifeline!

I have a friend who says she couldn't possibly wait for everything "to settle" before she has a moment or two for herself. She needs an hour or two before, during, and after the move so she can be nice to her family. Support Team Member Number 8 on her list is a massage therapist. She will travel anywhere if her husband promises this recovery therapy. She's noticed lately that this is a good way to spend time waiting for planes, as more international airports offer this service. "If only number eight for the kids and husband was also available at the same time!"

Men enjoy having a Number 8 on their personal support team, too. Some say, "I'll be fine once I find the golf course!"

Having a once-a-week Sabbath rest should also be about just resting! Take a moment to think about how you are going to take time off from all the planning, the organizing, and the stress of your move. The person on your support team that knows how to help you do this is important indeed.

Number 9: Financial Friend

This support team member is not your accountant, but someone who is happy to advise you on the prices of items you will need in your new location. This could be someone who is willing to go grocery shopping with you the first time, and tell you where to get the best deals. This person loves a bargain and is pleased to tell you where to find one or two yourself! Keep your ears tuned for the person who knows how to decorate a temporary home at good value, and ask if they have time to volunteer useful information on how and where to shop for your family.

Number 10: Housing Advisor

From day one, you will want to know who to call when the plumbing leaks or the telephone service fails to show up. Keep the number of this team member with you at all times, and remember them at Christmas! Check that any boiler you have has been serviced, and if there is anything you need to know to maintain your temporary home in good order.

Number 11: Driver

This personal support team member may not be someone who actually drives you anywhere, but he or she will know how to tell you to get places. If you can read maps, you may try to do this one yourself (or be on someone else's support team), but in the early days of living in any location, it's great to have a friend who doesn't mind a phone call for the "How do I get to…?" questions. Yes GPS is helpful, but sometimes there is just no replacing a human being with a map!

Number 12: Relocation or HR Advisor

The relocation or HR advisor is the person you call to answer your questions regarding what is covered or not covered in your relocation package. You may not need them often, but when you do they should be on-call to answer vital questions such as, "Is orthodontics covered in my medical plan when we are living here, or is this something I need to do back home?" or "Does our relocation package cover a trip home once a year?" You will, of course, have some idea as what your relocation package covers generally, but you may need to clarify specific questions regarding services for your family members. Your HR manager may be able to talk officially only to the employee, but keep the telephone number in case you need to have an informal chat. This person may be happy to assist you with various company spouse support initiatives (should there be any) and other matters that can be overlooked in the middle of a move. If you don't call them every other day, they are often more than happy to help.

Other than the first three on this list, the people and services mentioned are not in any order of importance. Part of the purpose of your research trip is to become aware of the support you will need. If you have your list in mind, you can be ready to ask people if they will be available to help you. I want to stress that it is important to ask Father God to set up divine appointments. He knows your needs and all you need to accomplish both on your research trip and after your move. He will bring people across your path. Space is provided where you can begin to line-up your own contact names and numbers (see Appendix F).

Always remember, *relocation is a team sport.*

Chapter Seven

GRANDMOTHERS AS COMMUNICATION CENTRAL

MIND THE GAP

A few years ago, my daughter was packing to head out on what the British call a Gap Year. This is a "year out," so to speak, for travel, work abroad, and simply taking time off the studies treadmill. The "kids" go when they finish secondary school at age 18, though more often the Gap Year is taken as my children did it, between undergraduate and grad school (Post Graduate School, as they say in the UK). These young people normally work for a few months to finance their flights, and then the parents pray over the credit card as they wave good-bye.

Not many people say too much about the reflective side of this year (that would be a little too embarrassing for young adult go-getters), but one of the subtle undercurrents of this year is that, for the young person concerned, it stops everyone from asking "what are you going to do in life?"

The early adult years in most countries are full of questions such as, "What are you studying? Are you job hunting? Thinking of university? What sports/social service are you doing? Will it look good on your college application?" These young people feel the pressure of not having answers.

As my daughter was sorting out her new backpack and thinking of warm clothes for Thailand, Malaysia, and Singapore, she was telling me that she had applied for permission to work in the outback of Australia. I listened intently.

I quietly prayed to God for strength to let her go. One or two members of my ladies group Bible study had already started regaling me with stories of prayers answered when their son or daughter was "on gap." Other members of this same group were actively praying for their children away on islands we never knew before existed (who would have thought of Raratonga as a place of grace?).

Sitting on the edge of my daughter's bed and mulling this over, the Holy Spirit suddenly gave me a thought that made me laugh out loud.

"What!" said Angela, who was prepared for my missing-you-already tears.

"Well…" I said, "I just had a picture of all those British grandmothers we hear about—the ones getting on the British Airways plane heading down to Sydney to see the grandkids and I wondered if one day I would be one of them!"

Teasingly, she put her arm around me, "After what you did to your mom, saying you'd only be away for two years in the Peace Corps, and now here you are with thirty years overseas…you would so deserve that!"

"But I'm only a hop over the pond from my parents. It takes twenty-four hours to fly to Australia!"

Angela gave me that "we're not having a serious conversation here are we?" look. I gave her a hug and said, "Well, I can pray you don't marry an Australian, can't I?"

"Closed!" she laughed. "This conversation is closed!"

Still, I beamed up a silent prayer that I had prayed since her conception. "Father, may she marry someone of Your choosing. Someone who loves You. And OK, whatever culture, even if it means me among the grandmas on the BA (air)bus to Sydney."

Angela completed her packing, and the whole family headed to the airport to see her off. Her brother cheered her on in anticipation of his own travels and her dad quietly hugged her and told her to have a great time. I was determined not to be like my mother and cry at airports, but oh, I did. Not too embarrassing, but embarrassing enough I suppose.

While Angela was traveling and experiencing life abroad, I felt God's strength and peace about what she was doing, but there was a gap in my heart. I missed her. I missed the phone calls from her college days, knowing I could send the chocolate chip cookies if she was having a tough week.

I missed too much to list, and I learned quite a lesson about being the one left behind. Years ago I had blithely left home and headed out on my own adventures for my very first job. With hardly a glance backward I had left my parents standing at Dulles International airport, waving at them and declaring, "Isn't this exciting!" I could hardly wait to start work that was anywhere but hometown.

My own mom had tried hard to hold back her airport tears, but couldn't. On the day I left, she said something about the fact she had been reading that many families had someone like me who needed to work in places that would let them see the world. "Would I be gone long?"

"Two years, mom. Just two years. Back before you know it." I clutched my Peace Corps acceptance papers.

Still, missionary families deal with this all the time. My aunt and uncle are with the Southern Baptist Missionary Board and to their parents, my grandparents, their relocating to Chile had seemed a long way from granddad's preaching in the small country churches in North Carolina. With all his sermons, why had it been the part about "going into all the world that had spoken to my aunt?" he said to me on one of our Lake Lure fishing trips.

And now, years later, I was the one to see that empty place at the dinner table. I was the one who expected my daughter to come home from college and dump the laundry; but instead, she was on the other side of the world.

When my son, Mark, headed for his gap year and decided he'd travel through Africa and sleep in a tent, I thought, "I don't have the courage for this." My ladies group would just have to permanently place me on the emergency prayer list. It's me O Lord, standing in the need of prayer would be my song every day he was away.

Mark, on the other hand, would be fine. He had the courage for these travels. He's a young man. He's on fire for the Lord! God told him he could go and that was all he needed to hear. It was me, Mark's mother, who had to pray for the courage to let go.

I later sat with Mark, blessedly back home, and watched the souvenir video of his time in Africa. There he was, full of peace while bungee jumping off Victoria Falls. Never had I seen a man do such a daring thing with such assurance in free fall. I'm so proud he did these things. He brought home stunning photography of moonlight over Namibia as well, and I give thanks that he was able to explore a quite remote part of the world. I am also (for the bungee jumping part) glad I wasn't there!

The travel bug spread throughout our family, and my niece, Elizabeth, decided she would take part in an American tradition of Junior Year abroad. She attended a school that I cannot for the life of me pronounce in guess where? Australia, of course. I suppose after all the years of Australian parents praying for their kids as they go "walkabout" through Europe and far off lands, it is only fair our kids return the favor and see their place.

They are not alone. Think of the mission teams that go abroad for one month to one year, or even 30 years. In airports all over America I see young people, and people of all ages, wearing matching mission team T-shirts and traveling to all the world.

GMAC's Global Relocation Trends 2009 tells us that about a third of multinational corporations believe there will be growth in their expatriate population1. People need to go where the jobs are. With all this coming and going, it can feel exciting to be part of a global nomadic world, but in this chapter I want to take a moment or two to consider the people we leave behind.

There is a gap, a disconnect, between those who go and those who stay.

My parents knew God wanted them to work at home while the kids were growing up, then felt the call to the mission field during their retirement years. At age 70-plus, they joined a team in South Korea and loved every minute of the three years they spent in Taejon. We were proud of them, but you have to hear the words of my sister, and how she felt as a young mother with her only child. Not everyone in a family thrives on an international lifestyle, and my sister wondered how her parents could put living and working in Korea over seeing their grandchild's first steps or first day at nursery school. As director of a hospital, my sister was not a stay-at-home mom, and she needed help that only a grandmother can give.

For one New York City senior banker, it was leaving behind his mother that proved a challenge. This grandmother *didn't want to miss* a single moment of her grandchildren growing up. She spent hours telling her son that they didn't leave "the old country" for him to be heading back to Europe so soon (two generations since Italy). It was only the promise of regular—and I mean monthly—flights with either the grandparents flying or the family flying back home, that convinced her that the family wouldn't fall apart.

Most of these conversations, especially with senior banking families, happen behind closed doors. It may be slightly embarrassing to have to deal with this issue. When you are sitting in internationally focused corporate meetings, it's not your best moment to admit that you might be part of a family that is not happy about its family members jetting off to far-flung places. One of my Jewish clients flew home from London to New York every Thursday to be back with his family in time for Shabbat. He was "so senior" as his personal assistant said, that no one argued. Just be a little "less senior" and try to do this.

Family ties that bind is an issue that can keep some people from even considering a move from one state to another, never mind thinking about an international relocation.

THE DISCONNECT

In the London Underground subway transportation system, there is often a space between the train and the station platform. Everyone knows that you have to take care when you step from the platform onto the train that is about to take off, but still we hear the announcement, "Mind the gap."

Who is minding the gap, looking after that space that is created between the platform, that launch-pad of home, and those on the train or plane? When the disconnection comes, what happens to those who remain in the home station?

Our family found one answer, not at an international conference, or from a globetrotting executive, or from a latest theory in cross-cultural communication, but deep in the Carolina foothills. The answer was new, and old as Jerusalem. Grandma was minding the gap. And she was doing it from her Methodist Wesley Pines retirement home.

MINDING THE GAP

While living in "independent living," my 80-plus years of age mother started scanning in and forwarding out and e-mailing prayer requests from and to any member of her family who was outside a 20-mile radius. While she prayed like every Christian grandmother has prayed for centuries, she became the communication support for those both home and away as only a 21st century grandmother could!

This grandmother in our family, my mother, was now home from her own travels. Her three years in South Korea and short stops in China and Australia among other places, helped her realize what it is like to be released by her family and to come home again. She has experienced the communication gap that happens with time zones and unshared adventures. She, with dad, stepped off the secure platform of home and boarded that plane and train that took them to Taejon. As a family, the rest of us had been left on the platform. The gap had felt like a gulf, she knew it; and she was determined to solve the disconnect that happens to families traveling and living overseas.

Jesus didn't have a lot of sympathy for those "left on the platform." I have often thought it was pretty harsh to say, as in Matthew and Luke to "let the dead bury their dead, but you follow Me" (see Matt. 8:22 and Luke 9:60). What about family?

Jill Southern, of Ellel Ministries, speaks on this issue when she says to members of the team at Pierrepont, England, "If God has called you to go to another place, another work for Him, *we*, like your family, *must hold you with an open palm.* We must find ways to support you with encouragement and prayer."

If someone has been called to go to another part of the world, those of us on the platform need to loosen any grip we might have and encourage freedom in Christ. We need to let them go, and cut off any ungodly ways that could possibly tie them to our plans and our purposes for their lives.

And though we let them go, we can mind the gap. Remember what I said earlier in this chapter about my daughter doing a gap year and working in Australia? I continued to pray a releasing prayer for her while she was away and I held her up to Father God for safekeeping.

One day I received a call from Australia. It was Angela. "Mom. I have something to tell you." (Silent prayer now happening in my mind that calls on the name of Jesus). " I have met someone…"

She let me hang on the phone for a very long and expensive minute. "And he's from Manchester, England!" she laughed, knowing exactly what she had done to me! I listened intently again, and was very happy to hear that she wasn't getting married in the outback but was heading back to the UK with a new friend.

"Isn't it amazing" she said, "that Dave, my friend I'm telling you about, will be going to the same grad school as me?"

"Oh yes, amazing," I said, smiling as I could almost hear the Holy Spirit say to me "Trust Me *now?*"

"And isn't it amazing that Dave is a Christian who wants a girlfriend who is committed to doing things God's way in dating?"

"Oh my, even more amazing." Silent tears were now streaming my face.

"Well. We'll see what happens. He and I will just have to see if we still want to go out with each other when we get to Oxford. Can't believe he'll be at Oxford Brooks, same as me."

"Oh, I'm beginning to believe more," I almost said, but instead just said I loved her and looked forward to meeting her at the airport.

"Wait till you see my great tan," she said.

"Wait till you see my big embarrassing Welcome Home banner."

It's not easy being left behind, but we do need to hold our loved ones on open palms. There is freedom in following Christ, and it was for freedom that He came. If He tells a family member, or close friend, or mission team member, or work colleague that they are to go somewhere new, who are we to hold them back?

We can ask them questions. We can ask if they are sure the Father told them to go, and how has He confirmed this direction in their lives. We can ask, and we can listen to their answers and pray that they have clarity regarding the God's plans and purposes for their life, but we cannot stand in their way.

We can recognize the gap that is there when this loved one is gone from our lives, even temporarily. Then we need to ask God how we can be spiritually minded about this gap. How can we keep communication going? How can we pray? How can we practically support them?

Ask God to send the Holy Spirit to stand in the gap; it's what Jesus did when He was just about to head home.

CREATIVE GAP MINDING

Is someone in your family, or someone close to you, about to leave? Are you the one left behind? If so, take a moment to read this prayer and see if you can pray these things in your heart:

Father God, in the name of Jesus I come to You. I place _____ on the open palm of my hand and release _____ into Your plans and purposes for his/her life. I lift all my concerns for safety for spirit, soul and body to You. Place a hedge of protection around _____ and cover _____ by the blood of Jesus. Please show me if there is anything I am doing or saying that would stand in his/her way of carrying out what You want _____ to do. May the Holy Spirit fill any gap in my heart that I experience. Guide me in how to pray for _____ in the days to come. In Jesus' name alone, Amen.

Are you the one going?

Father God, in the name of Jesus I come to You. Thank You that Your son Jesus Christ would only do what You, the Father, did and set an example of praying that workers would be sent out to the harvest field. Thank You for sending me to _____. I ask that You cut off any ungodly ties I may have to home, friends, or work and strengthen the godly ties. Pull me out from under the influence of anything that would stand in the way of Your plan and purpose for my life, and fill in the gap with the presence of Your Holy Spirit. Help me to say good-bye in any manner You choose and to have compassion on all those who do not understand why I am leaving. Keep all who I leave behind safe in the knowledge and love of Christ. In Jesus' name alone, Amen.

Take a moment to write your own thoughts or prayer about either being left behind or leaving someone behind. Ask the Holy Spirit to inspire you to mind the gap in ways that nurture your spirit.

_____
_____
_____
_____
_____

These prayers are based on Ellel Ministries teaching on the NETS course. For more information regarding courses, healing retreats and events, please visit: www.Ellelministries.org.

Chapter Eight

EXPECTING AND DELIVERING
A BABY ABROAD

My husband sat mesmerized at the computer. "Have a look at this," he said with not a little awe in his voice. There before us was one of the most amazing e-mail attachments I have ever seen in my life, a baby only months old *in the womb*. We could see every limb, a tiny head and big belly, and then the baby moved! The scan of this precious child rotated around his little body and allowed us a marvelous glimpse of new life that was coming into our family hundreds of miles away in Italy. My husband was about to be a grandfather, again.

Between us, Christopher and I have six kids. Three of his children and my two live in the United Kingdom, but his second daughter, Alison, lives with her husband, Giovanni, in a small town on the Adriatic coast of Italy. This would be his first grandchild born in another country.

Global nomads have new tools in the toolbox when it comes to sharing the latest family news, but it is not just high-tech baby scans or Skype phone calls or even Web cams that allow military kids to see their parent in Afghanistan, or corporate parents to connect with grandparents while on business in New York, or missionary kids in Mozambique to connect with school in Kansas (or the other way around!) that is a cause for celebration. Every time I see creative technology enabling families to connect and communicate, I give thanks. We need every technology tool available, and we will need to get even more creative as we see our little ones born into a vastly changing world. There are few "How to be a Global Parent" books and few "older, wise women" stepping up to the plate to teach younger moms in the international arena. It is my hope that this chapter is a help to all who are preparing to have babies a long way from home. Listen as women share their experiences with you.

So What Is it Like to Have a Baby in Another Country?

Jo is from England and, like my step-daughter Alison, she moved to Italy several years ago with her husband, but she already had two kids. It wasn't long before she was pregnant with her third child. When it's your third or fourth pregnancy, it's easy to think you just have to get on with things and not take care to rest as you should. With the move to a fairly rural location, spending time grape picking, olive picking, and setting up her new home, Jo went into premature labor at 28 weeks.

"I hardly knew any Italian at the time, but I went to the local hospital," said Jo. "The woman in the next bed told me that I needed to be transferred to the regional hospital if it looked like I needed a special baby unit. Everyone was so nice at the local hospital that I didn't want to go, but finally I did request a transfer for the sake of the baby. They were wonderful and even sent a doctor and a nurse to ride with me in the ambulance for the hour's journey. I had to say good-bye to the local hospital staff as soon as we arrived at the regional medical center."

"At this larger hospital, the staff was not as nice, and I wondered if I had made a mistake. Rachel, my baby, was born, and they whisked her off to the special unit. I wanted to hold Rachel, but they wouldn't let me. Finally I just asked 'why?' and they explained that they were not thinking about me, but about the baby. They saved her life and I have to say all is well now. She is sharp as a pin!"

"It wasn't long before I had my fourth child," Jo continued, "and had a very straight forward labor, but this time I knew a little more of the language and understood some of the cultural differences. For example, Italian doctors think they are god. They want to speak over you and not look you in the eye. I just kept looking right at my doctor and made him look at me! You have to have a sense of humor. This expat life is a good life but a hard life. If you can't turn around and say to certain cultural differences 'this is ridiculous!' you'll go under! You have to be able to laugh. You have to ask 'why is this different?' I just knew I wanted a real conversation with my doctor and we finally got there. I even amazed his nurses!"

Lisa from California recalls several years of not being able to conceive and even now recognizes the need for emotional healing for that time in her life. "I just couldn't understand why this was happening to me, but I learned to pray without ceasing! I met up with several other women at the American Women's group for Bible Study. We regularly prayed that my husband and I would be able to have a child, and when we succeeded, those women all celebrated and became honorary aunts! My son has an honorary aunt from at least ten states!"[1]

Mary and Tim from Florida had their first child while living overseas in Singapore. They loved knowing that the doctors would tell them exactly what to do; but even more Mary enjoyed the post-natal exercises that happened daily in the hospital. "I felt like I was on a cruise ship!" she recalled.[2]

My mother-in-law gave birth on a British military base in Germany, which as she was German would have been fine but her English wasn't that great at the time and *at that* particular time, Germans were not the flavor of the month with the British. A friend of mine, the wife of an IBM employee, insisted on going back to India to give birth. Her father was a doctor at the hospital and that is where she wanted to be. Some people get to pick and choose where they will give birth and others don't. We don't all get the smooth, your wish is my command, birthing experience.

There are so many stories of childbirth in far lands, and young moms have anecdotes that range from "Paris is a great place to give birth—but not in August. All the doctors are on vacation!" to tips on the best locations for home and natural birth. To hear more stories where moms and dads compare notes on having a child abroad, including adoption and support for children with special needs, visit the Website listing in the chapter Endnotes.

SCRIPTURES FOR THE ROAD

Have you just learned that you are relocating to a new region or country? Have you just learned that you are pregnant? Welcome to the story of Mary, the mother of Jesus. Even thinking about riding on that donkey makes me start praising Father God for airline tickets. I wonder now at the wisdom and knowledge Mary had as she rode to Bethlehem. You need that rock solid peace in your heart as the Shepherd leads you gently in the details of your move. This is trust. Your very words and attitude will make evident your Source of peace and wisdom. Preparing your mind to have an attitude of gratitude is true preparation!

Your Father God will give you "Scriptures for the road." These will be verses just for you, to give you peace, to give you certain knowledge that He is there for you every step of your pregnancy. Purchase the slimmest little travel Bible you can find, and make sure it is in your carry-on travel bag. Scribble down the Scriptures He gives you specifically for your pregnancy, labor, and travel plans. Keep them in your pockets or purse. Get them out every moment imaginable and declare them in your heart and mind and even aloud. Whether you are happy and excited about the move or dreading it, your attitude will determine your peace during this life-changing event.

PREPARING TO RECEIVE WISDOM

As you are depositing Scripture deep down inside your spirit, you will be nurturing your spirit and guarding your heart. This is essential for establishing a "plumb line" for what you hear at your personal watering well. As you listen to stories or ask questions about childbirth from women you respect, line up all they say with the Word of God. Be prepared to discern that what is said is what you need to hear!

While there is wisdom in seeking counsel from older and experienced women, you need to use God's Word to set a boundary around your mind. The role of women passing down information is to be welcomed, but do not welcome all that is said. Be prepared to receive and to not receive.

As you get dressed in the morning, put on the whole armor of God piece by piece. When it comes to the shield, remind yourself to put up that shield to stop information or stories that would set fear into your mind, will, or emotions. Receive wisdom and knowledge that serve the purpose of reassuring you that you can go where the Lord leads and do what He asks you to do.

Anytime someone tells what I call a "fear story," put your hand (your shield) up just slightly, as a way of reminding yourself that while you might be polite to whomever is telling you some crazy child-birth story (what they believe to be wisdom!), you are not receiving this into your spirit! It is also a good idea to "pray off your mind" anything that you know is not from God. Just say, "Father, I want to receive all that You have for me, but if it is not for me to receive (a story or advice), then let it go completely from my mind. In Jesus' name, Amen."

Susan's experience is a good example of what I am talking about. In the same week she learned that she was pregnant, her husband announced that his work was sending them to England. They had both hoped for this pregnancy and for a work transfer to southern England, but the timing was a little unexpected to say the least. Suddenly, at all the watering holes (church, Starbuck's, doctor's office, and neighborhood gatherings), women had stories to tell and they were not great stories. Most of what she was told was meant to discourage her from going to England while she was pregnant. She was told horrific tales about socialized medicine and how she would have no say in the type of labor she wanted. Thankfully, for Susan's sake, she had set her course by knowing that this relocation was an answer to prayer and she could trust God for the plans He had for them. To say that she had a good birthing experience would be a British understatement; so much so, she began to hope they would have their second child while living in their small town in Oxfordshire. Is the British National Health system perfect? Not by a long shot. Is this to say that we should ignore words of caution about having a baby in another country? Not at all. Let caution and warning be the basis of research; just don't assume that someone else's experience will be your experience.

Preparing to receive wisdom is preparing to set a guard over your mind. Set what can be called a "hedge of protection" concerning all that you choose to hear. Ask God for discernment regarding wise counselors, particularly determining if anyone for any reason could share deception. The loveliest and most innocent people who in no way mean you harm, can share information that is not helpful. Wisdom is to know how to answer them and not let fear enter your heart.

Knowledge is the facts you need to know for the birth of your child. Wisdom is knowing who to listen to and what facts to take on board. Pray for the wisdom to discern the knowledge you need.

KNOWLEDGE

There are three types of knowledge, or information, that you need to gather as you prepare to give birth.

1. *Biological:* Let's start with the women in your own family. As labor trends come and go, focus not just on the "how to have a baby" type of information, but stories of your family's

genetic heritage. Has anyone had diabetes? Any problems giving birth? Any history of a genetic disorder? Is there a history of miscarriage in your family; and if yes, at what month? Ask your husband's mother about her birthing experience. Is there anything you need to know regarding health issues that might possibly be passed down along the generational line? Some genetic problems are passed down along the female line, and some only in the male line. This information can help you decide whether or not your doctor in your new location has the expertise you need.

2. *Emotional:* Ask your mother if she had any post-partum depression. If your mother doesn't want to discuss these issues, ask an aunt or long time family friend. If baby blues runs in your family, you and your husband can be prepared spiritually, emotionally, and physically. Is there a tradition in your family of a grandparent coming to stay for a few days (a month?) to give support and assist with looking after the baby? Who will be on the other end of the telephone when you need emotional support? All being well, how do you and your husband plan to support each other at this exciting, but often challenging time? If you have other children, who will help you look after them while you are in the hospital? How do you plan to prepare your older children for the newest member of your family?

3. *Spiritual:* I will talk about praying for your child, but the focus here is to gather information regarding faith-based traditions in your and your husband's family. Are you hoping to have a christening just months after the birth of your child? Do you prefer a more informal dedication? What about circumcision? Do you have prayer support for all the stages of a healthy and happy pregnancy and birth?

SHARING STORIES

From ancient times, women have gathered at the well, barn raisings, sewing circles, Starbucks to share their stories with each other. We were designed to share wisdom. We were made to compare notes and pass on practical knowledge that encourages us to love our husbands and raise strong families. We aren't meant to gossip, but we are meant to share information that will help us *do family life.* As Father God has entrusted women to give birth, He also gave us the gift of networking and sharing information that is vital to new life.

You need to find women in your new location (see chapter Endnote 3 for helpful Websites) who have recently given birth and ask them, "Which hospitals are the best?" and "What makes them the best?" Who are the good doctors? What is it like to have a local midwife deliver your baby? See if there are women in your new church who will share their birthing stories with you, so you can have an understanding of any cultural differences that may affect the choices you make regarding labor or care of your newborn.

While you need the biological, emotional, and spiritual information and wisdom from the older women in your family, you need to blend this source of knowledge with that of women your own age who are also starting or growing their families. This is where technology can be of real help.

DO YOUR RESEARCH

If you still aren't convinced about the importance of the Internet when it comes to globally connected family life, then please let me encourage you to at least use it to do a little research as you prepare to have a baby. Level Fours won't need this encouragement, you just about live on the Internet, and you will have the great fun of checking out a variety of cultural approaches to childbirth as well as asking relatives and friends around the world how their labor was in Indonesia, Cambodia, or Los Angeles.

If you are a Level Seven reading this in the privacy of your closet so that no one will ever know you might in a weak moment, connect with "home thinking" or "culture of origin thinking" (global nomad speak!) then let me be clear. The reason for research is, quite simply, pain. Yes, pain or, more specifically, *pain relief.*

It may come as a surprise to you that not all OBGYN doctors believe in pain relief for labor. While some doctors, American and European, have elevated this discussion to a philosophy of "rites of passage for womanhood," it comes down to the fact that some state or public hospitals (with free care) do not offer pain relief of any sort during labor and if you want the pain relief option, you may well need to go private.

Corporate and military wives may sigh with relief at their medical package, but many women reading this book will be heading to mission fields or helping start up a family business in major cities, and doctors and hospitals can be quite expensive.

Please don't misunderstand me. I see natural childbirth as a wonderful "rite of passage" for women. After my son's birth (in the UK), I remember thinking to myself that there would now be no need to climb Mount Everest. I would leave that to the poor men who never had a chance in the course of their lives to test themselves to the limit as I had in childbirth. Yet, my daughter took twenty-four hours to deliver. I was exhausted and the medical staff became concerned that I had no physical resources left to give birth. They gave me an epidural so that I could have a few hours to recover, and then stopped it at the point of delivery. Without the pain relief break (or option of caesarean) it is very likely one of us would have died. I praise God and give thanks that though I was not a private patient, I had options for pain relief, a competent and caring staff, and a quiet room with home-like lighting and my music. The operating room was seconds down the corridor if all went a little too wild for me or the baby. Pray for Father God to be in the details of your labor.

When you are pregnant, many women begin dreaming of the type of labor they would like to have. For example, home births, special baby unit births, hospital birth with a midwife, birthing in a bath. There are so many choices from a global perspective, but you will need to know what is offered wherever you will be living. That's where blogs and chat rooms enable other mothers and sometimes fathers to share vital information on giving birth from Paris to Penang. Do the research and know the availability and cost of the medical care you need.

Know Your Level of Relocation

After reading Chapter 2 and deciding the Level of Relocation you wish to make, you may find that becoming a parent changes everything. People, who are comfortable with Level One or Level Two moves, often prefer to head home for giving birth. Just remember that airlines have deadlines for allowing you to fly. Remember, also, that this choice often means a period of separation between you and your husband, if he needs to head back to work before you and the baby are ready to travel. Whenever you are ready to travel with your baby, even if you do not go home for the birth, you need to remember to get your baby a passport and these days that means showing up in person at the passport office with your newborn.

If heading home is impossible for whatever reason, you can make your environment look and feel like the next best thing. Look again at the Web-sites provided in the Endnotes, and start your research!

Level Three and Four mothers often like to head to the nearest major city to give birth. We, and I say we because I was living a Level Six life when I was pregnant and became much happier when I realized I needed to gather a multicultural Level Four life around me. Level Three and Four mothers enjoy researching how women give birth in a variety of cultures and then take what suits us to make the birth experience our own. A typical Level Three or Four mother will want, for example, American technology available, but a British midwife who is great without the technology, and then a German lullaby with low lights in the birthing room, and the warmth and strength of a Jamaican grandmother to tell us that she has seen it all before and that "you'll be fine," and then a Chinese grandmother to bring lunch, and then back to the American scene where dinner is served to new mom and dad in their private room on the night before they go home from the hospital. We don't want much!

Level Five, Six, and Seven mothers just want to know how the new location provides for birth and new babies, and in the course of getting to know the local people they often select to fit into "local ways and means" as much as possible. Level Five mothers enjoy giving birth in multiple locations (OK, that's three or four children!), and thrive on memories of "when I was in Tokyo we had Andrew and they had wonderful nurses!" and then when they change countries it's, "and when we were in Cape Town we had Mark and a lovely woman gave me the best breastfeeding support." These robust Level Five moms adapt everywhere they go, and this easy adaptation is partly because they know each country of residence is only temporary. If one culture isn't to their liking; well, they will soon be on their way to yet another location. It may be total immersion into the culture of the moment; but for Level Five ladies, life is one big tapestry of adventures.

Level Six and Level Seven mothers, often prefer the new culture over their home culture when it comes to having children. Though my step-daughter Alison can see some advantages (especially financial) to having a baby in England, she likes the lifestyle in Italy, and this is where she wants to give birth. She isn't interested in heading home (Level One or Two desire), or getting those of her own nationality and other nationalities around her at the time of pregnancy (Level Four), unless it is her own mother or immediate family.

Trouble comes when a woman who thought she was a Level Six or Seven suddenly changes her mind about her desired Level of Relocation when she becomes pregnant. You need to be honest with yourself, and your husband, if you think this has happened, or is happening in the course of pregnancy, or even after birth. I know many Level Six women who changed quite dramatically after the baby arrived. More than one American mom, having given birth quite happily overseas, suddenly started dreaming of yellow school buses!

Remember, when you can't change countries, change levels! You may find that even temporarily changing your level of living overseas gives you comfort and peace. Re-read the levels in Chapter 2 and consider ways you can adapt your level to your changing needs.

PRAYING FOR AND FROM CONCEPTION

One of the most important things you can do for your about-to-be-born child is to pray for him or her. Just as you start preparing your body for pregnancy with good nutrition and for labor by researching your options, so you can prepare yourself and the baby spiritually. Pray for a godly conception (even after the fact) where your child receives nourishment and love right from the start. As you pray for this time when your baby is in the womb, pray for his or her protection in spirit, soul, and body. Do a little proactive spiritual warfare, and come against any spirit of rejection. Declare good things over this child from the very beginning of life.

Pray for the medical team who will be looking after you and for all preparations for birth. Pray that your baby will be ready (including positioning in the womb), according to God's timing for birth, and pray for ways in which you can receive your child with love beyond measure. Pray that your baby will know in his or her little spirit that they are a much loved and welcomed child into your family.

COACH, COUNSELOR, CHEERLEADER

In the early days of your newborn's life you will find that you need a new type of support for you, your husband, and the baby. You know all about the wisdom of listening to knowledge that can help with pregnancy and labor, but now you need guidance for enabling your little one to thrive. You may have loads of family coming to visit, all packed with advice they are ready to dish out—or you may have the expat community at your side. You may have the women of your church visiting you and bringing a meal or two. You may be totally on your own in Brussels or Winchester, and your husband is in Hong Kong.

Whether among people or feeling a little isolated in and among your attempts to find an hour or so of sleep, you need to be on the look out for three types of people who will help you focus on the baby's needs. You need a coach or two, a counselor, and at least one cheerleader.

Coach

A coach is someone with skill. They have knowledge that will make your life thrive! One coach I know is a personal (to me) joy when it comes to shopping. He is an older member of our church, and a pharmacist. Any item you plan to buy, you can always check out with Wesley, and he will tell you whether or not there are unsafe chemicals in the product. Someone like Wesley is very handy to know when it comes to buying your first baby food, especially when you can't recognize a single brand name.

A coach you will especially want in the first few days after giving birth is someone who can support you with breastfeeding. Breastfeeding gives an infant vital immunities and will give you precious bonding time with your baby. While many cultures support nursing, some hospital nurses actively discourage it, and you need to know whom to turn to for support. Check the La Leche Website[4] for online information and sources of support.

A third coach to look for is someone who has sound advice regarding sleep for both you and your baby. There are a variety of theories when it comes to those all important hours of sleep, and I have listed in Endnote 5 Websites that have differing approaches. Both parents should look at these Websites and discuss the approach best suited for your family. Sleep often requires teamwork!

Counselor

A counselor is someone you can talk to about the joys and problems arising from having a baby far from home. As parents, you need to be supportive of each other's needs at this time, but it is wise to be on the look out for anyone Father God might send your way to give you insights into the early days of parenting. One counselor we had reminded us of the need to pray for our babies and in the midst of changing diapers and feeding it was like a revelation. You can get very busy indeed, and a counselor is someone who helps you not only establish priorities for family life, but looks for ways that help you keep those priorities. Counseling at its best helps you meet your goals for you and the new addition to your family. These days no one is allowed to call themselves a counselor unless they have a professional qualification and some legal document to hang on the wall, but counselors in the biblical sense are always available if you ask God to send them to you.

Cheerleader

My father was my cheerleader. The moment he stepped off the plane to visit my husband and I and our first baby, you could see the pride in his eyes. As my love language is words of encouragement,[6] it filled my heart with peace to hear him say "Kathy, you are such a good mother."

Grandparents make great cheerleaders, so do sisters and brothers or a mid-wife who helped you deliver the baby. A cheerleader is someone who sees something of value in your parenting and lets you know! A cheerleader is not the one who evaluates your parenting or teaches you necessarily, but one who encourages you to be the best mother or father you can be. Fathers need to hear someone say, "You're a great dad!" or "It's wonderful how you are so proud of your baby."

Try not to be too proud to find a cheerleader. The Bible calls us to be encouragers, but it sometimes takes a little humility to receive encouragement. Look for the natural encouragers in your life, the ones who are gifted in this area. You are not looking for flattery, but for someone to help you stir up your faith and share the joy of new life. Your cheerleader will encourage you both, as new parents, to receive all that Father God intends you to receive, enabling you to carry out the plans and purpose of your family life.

THE HOLY SPIRIT

If you have given your life to the Lord Jesus Christ, you have the promise that you will lack for nothing. Sometimes we do not have, because we do not ask; but if we ask, He will send coaches. He will be your counselor and show you ways to stir up your spirit. He can *be* Coach, Counselor, and

Cheerleader in one. Ask God for divine appointments wherever you give birth to your baby, and ask Him to give you eyes to see what or who is sent by Him. Ask Him for ears to hear what you need to hear and a divine deafness to all that is not helpful. Ask Him for favor with doctors, nurses, and for your delivery. Ask Him for the peace of the Lord to bless you. Above all, give thanks, especially if you are not traveling on a donkey to an inn with no room. Give thanks and welcome that new little life!

Chapter Nine

HEADING HOME—HEADING OUT AGAIN

Standing on the dock of Southampton Harbour, I looked up and gazed at the very large and beautiful QE II. High above, Carol and her husband, Tony, the two boys and even their newborn daughter were waving flags and yelling "Thank you! Good-bye. Come see us!" (OK. Well, the daughter was just cooing, smiling, and probably wondering what all the fuss was about.)

I stood back from the dockside crowd of well-wishers and had another look at the people from a small village in Dorset who had come for the send off. Only moments before I had actually been on the ship saying a personal good-bye to this American family and sharing some fun memories of when they had arrived in England just three years earlier.

"Remember," said Carol, "when we were visiting all those schools and I said I didn't believe you that saying good-bye would be harder than moving here?"

We laughed and my mind flashed back to the first days Carol's school run and being the only American mother at a lovely English school. "And you said," I reminded her, "that from the moment you wake up until the moment you went to bed, everything you did in this culture was wrong."

"And it was!" she said. "I didn't know that you don't give big presents to teachers at Christmas and one mother thought I was trying bribe the teacher, and the vocabulary! I now know what exercise books are…and holidays like Boxing Day…"

"And look at the friends you have made, the families who love you and have come to say good-bye. You are going to be missed."

This Long Island, New York, couple had made great efforts to get to know the families of their son's classmates. Though they had only Level One experience in relocation (none!) they had a Level Six ability for fitting in and becoming part of this very English culture. As testimony to this, there was quite a group who had taken time off work to come and give them a "proper send off" with a huge homemade banner proclaiming, MISSING YOU ALREADY. English voices mimicking Long Island accents shouted these words as the boat was about to set sail.

Carol and Tony, in addition to the work that Tony had carried out for the bank, had been what I call grass root diplomats. Though they were not alleviating poverty in this wealthy area of the world, I considered the cross-cultural friendships they made to be worthy of a Peace Corps badge. Not that there is one!

Still, whenever people from one nation live among people of another nation and build bridges of understanding, it goes along way to undoing the damage done on the evening news. Many newscasts build walls between nations and Carol and Tony, just by their lives as a family, broke down some of the prejudice of one nation against another.

Again and again, people in England had said to them, "You have a gun, right?"

"No," Carol would say.

"I thought all Americans had guns. I saw a program on TV and it was just dreadful how you Americans have guns."

"I don't own one," Carol would say, realizing that she was becoming the spokesperson for all America. Whenever something had been said about her country on the news the night before, she would be asked for verification the next day.

Through Carol and Tony's ability to be open and discuss whatever came up at dinner parties, daily school life, and church events, they had simply made friends. Carol admitted she did find it difficult to not be upset when someone said something uncomplimentary about America, but she tried to be a polite guest in another person's home country.

"And look at me now," she said. "I want to go home and I don't want to go home. Living in Europe means you can travel and see places like Italy and go skiing in France and offer the kids amazing experiences. Going home kind of feels like the party is over. I am going to miss the expat life."

ALL CHANGE

As mentioned previously, my mother-in-law changed countries 21 times. That's the British Army, at least in the days after World War II. She had been a German translator for the British forces, and married an English soldier. Her moving meant 21 houses, 21 times of packing and unpacking boxes and babies, not to mention 21 changes of address and settling in the children.

"Still, we had it easier than young families do today," she said. Thinking that she meant the army had it all organized compared to the more isolated moves of the corporate world, I asked her to tell me more. I was quite surprised at her response.

"We didn't do our change of country so quickly. Nowadays, a young family packs up and flies out. In twenty-four hours you have changed everything and you do not give yourself anytime to process where you left and think about where you are going."

In the 1950s and even the '60s, army families often moved to their new country by ship. On board they had time to talk to other people relocating to India or Cyprus, even if the troops had gone on ahead. During this time, letters (remember those?) could be written, thoughts updated in journals, and conversations with at least the youngest children could enable a family to process the adjustments that needed to be made to a new country and bring closure to what they were leaving behind.

Today I often recommend to families that they cruise home (OK, that's *my* dream!), or at least take a few days vacation "between countries," so they can process the leaving behind (closure) and manage expectations of what is ahead (transition), even if the next country is the country of origin for some members of the family.

CLOSURE

There are some things everyone has to do to get ready to leave a country, and there are some things that depend on both the Relocation Level you have been living and the time you have been overseas. Closure means saying good-bye. Take time to say it properly, and you and your family will reap the reward of maximum emotional health for what is a stressful event by anyone's standards. Let's look at what needs to be done first.

THE WRAP UP

If you go back to the strategic priorities discussed in Chapter 1, you won't make a move without checking with Father God. Has He opened doors for your leaving? Has He made it clear that it is time to go?

If the Holy Spirit has prompted you in your spirit to prepare for a move, you will need to start what I call "godly closure." This isn't just about leaving the place better than you found it, but to spend some time asking Jesus, "How should I do this? How do I leave this place? Order my footsteps, please."

If your stay in the country you are just about to leave has not been a good experience, there is something to be said about just wiping your feet and moving on. In other words, look at any ties you have made with the people and the place. Ask Father God to strengthen in any way He sees fit all that was good about your time in this location, and to cut you off from all that was not good. Ask Him to supernaturally have the Holy Spirit bring you out from under any negative influence for you and your family while living here.

Even if living in this location was a good experience, do the same. Your Father God can be amazingly creative in showing you how to strengthen ties to people and places that may live large in your memory. Invite Him to heal any damage that you may have been unaware of to your spirit and soul.

Ideally, take a few days to go away and pray through this time as a family. Listen to each other and ask Father God to give you discernment about how to be wise in protecting your family in spirit, soul, and body for leaving this country and heading home or heading out to yet another country or region.

If you are facing a "Three Week Wonder" (that is *all* the notice you get for making this move), then do what I call a "Susanna Wesley." Susanna had 12 kids and zero time to herself. She, however, was not daunted by this fact, or her overly busy pastor husband, and would sit in the middle of the room and pull her hooped skirt over her head for a little private prayer time. You may be fresh out of hooped skirts, but you can lock the loo (bathroom) and have ten minutes to yourself!

Let your Father God know exactly how you feel about this move. This could be "Thank You, thank You, thank You!" or it could be, "*How* am I going to say good-bye to _____!?" Whatever your situation, take a moment if not a weekend, to start connecting your emotions to the facts of this next relocation.

Departing Testimony

So, how are you going to wrap up this time in a way that gives a testimony to your faith? Many people give a double clean to their house so that when the next person moves in they do not say disparaging things about their nationality. They want everyone to know that (fill in your own nationality) people are clean and tidy and know how to take care of a house.

Of course, some people could care less and just leave the house behind in a condition that is less than considerate. "Why should I bother?" ask some who find packing too much trouble, even when the moving company does it all for them. "You should have seen it when I got here!" they say.

My mother-in-law doesn't have fond memories of the 21 houses she moved into that needed an immediate spring cleaning, but she left each of her houses in an immaculate state. Some people just need to be told to leave a house ready for the next family to arrive.

As a Christian or family of faith, think about how you can bless the next family who will be moving into the house where you have been living. After a thorough clean, how about praying through each room and asking the Holy Spirit to bring His fragrance and cleanse it of any times of acrimony or of any activity that was not a good witness to the love of Jesus.

Not only should the house be as clean as possible, how about some notes on the kitchen table which include a list of local churches, and even telephone numbers for pizza delivery or the addresses of local restaurants that your family has enjoyed? How about one or two toiletries or dishwashing liquid? Do I need to mention toilet paper in the toilets, and light bulbs that work? Ask Jesus, "How can I bless this family who is coming along next?"

Children's Calendar

Two lovely ladies, Dr. Jill Crystal and Hazel Stoddard[1] have worked in this area of assisting children as they prepare to relocate. One of the items they make is the Relocation Calendar for Children. This is a special "children's own" calendar, complete with stickers for each step of the packing and moving process.

If you have time, make your own calendars with stickers for the day "the movers" arrive, the last day of school, the day you have a good-bye party, and other days you want to highlight. You can, of course, give each of the children their own individual calendar, personalizing it with either stickers or written notes.

PARTIES

Good-bye parties are emotionally exhausting for the whole family. I suggest you have separate children's and adult's parties, but that may be because I've always had a joint venture. When everyone is together, it is hard to concentrate on emotional needs, but at least proper good-byes are said.

Make a speech, a few personal words that say you recognize you have been blessed by friendships. *Try* not to tell everyone you meet that you are inviting them to "come to Dubai" or wherever it is you are going. Do have a guest book passed around for everyone to note their contact details, and make a point of sending Christmas cards at least for the first year. After that, you will know who your lasting friends are and those who were great for just a season.

Large or small, parties are a way of acknowledging the role others have played in your lives in this location, and to say thank you. A party acknowledges closure.

FINAL, FINAL GOOD-BYES

I prefer to then meet up with a close friend or two for coffee or lunch just before or after the good-bye party. My Connecticut walking partner, Marlene, and I went for a "last walk," stopping at Maggie's Station House on Main Street for a last cappuccino. We still try to organize a good walk every couple of years!

I never say good-bye to family members. As we don't live in the same town even when we are all in the same country, I can live with the illusion that living in another country is just like living in another state. I am still coming home for Thanksgiving!

RECORDING SPEECH

Record your children talking before you leave home. Do it again before you head home or on to another location. It's lovely for everyone to see how accents change or manner of speaking changes over time and location. My daughter especially had the most incredibly posh English accent before we left Winchester, England, and she firmly announced in her recording that year that it would "never change!" It took her about a month before she was a real-sounding New Englander.

I've noticed over the years, that the rate of change a child makes with their accent matches the rate they are settling into their new school. Try it and see if you agree.

Many years ago a family asked me to meet with them after their move from England to America. Every child in the family had settled in well, except one daughter whom I will call Kirsty. Kirsty was 10 and was wetting the bed. I agreed to an informal visit to see if a chat could determine what the problem was.

I arrived at their beautiful and spacious home, and the girls gave me the guided tour. "It's cool!" they said, and excitedly showed me the new computer and the huge "rec room." They loved all the home gadgets. They demonstrated how to speak into an intercom system in the kitchen that "dinner was ready" and the announcement would reach every bedroom. Cool!

As I listened to the girls talk about their friends in school and declare that the neighborhood was "a great place for riding my bicycle," I noticed that three of the four girls had newly acquired American accents, and the fourth girl, Kirsty, was still solidly English.

We gathered in the dining room for the evening meal. Dad was home by now and he was fun to watch with his daughters. They obviously adored him. He scooped up the youngest in his arms, and hugged the older girls. He inquired after their day, and it was clear that this was a daily event with his children. This was not show for my sake. They loved him and he loved them. The mother was a little more gentle, but kind and loving as well. I couldn't get a feel for what was going wrong for Kirsty. Maybe she was being bullied at school?

While I made a mental note to visit her classroom, the mother started dishing out the meal and passing plates around. This larger than life dad began telling the girls about his day. As he held forth, I began to get a picture as to what was going wrong for Kirsty. Her dad was laughing and telling jokes, but he was mostly ridiculing every American he had met that day. He laughingly asked one of his daughters to "say something." This daughter said a sentence with her new accent and they all had a laugh together. "My daughter used to sound educated," he said. I looked at this daughter, and she was having a great time and teased him back about something that had changed in him.

I then looked at Kirsty. She was not laughing. Kirsty toyed with her food and quietly excused herself from the table at the first possible moment. "See?" said the mother quietly to me.

After dinner, the parents and I went to the kitchen for a chat while the girls headed off to do homework. "What do you think?" they asked. After checking that all was well with Kirsty at school, I said I had an idea.

I suggested that while Kirsty seemed to adore her father, she might not be sure she had permission to "become American" for the time they were here. We brainstormed some ways in which the father could reassure Kirsty that he would not have brought her to a place, *or at least stayed in a place* that he thought would harm her. He needed to make America an emotionally safe place for Kirsty. She needed to know that she would not be ridiculed if she chose to adapt to her new surroundings. The family agreed to try a new approach at the dinner table conversation for a month, and see what happened. It was amazing the difference that month made to Kirsty. Her accent changed, she began to make friends, and the bedwetting stopped.

A few weeks later, the dad made a point of spending some time alone with Kirsty, playing a little "soccer." As he kicked the ball her way, he said, "You know I was only joking."

"Now I do," she said and ran a few rings around him with the ball. This time she smiled.

More recently, the family returned home. It took about six weeks for all accents to change back, but they had learned something about making change an emotionally safe adventure within the family.

PHOTO ALBUM

Hopefully, you will have been taking some photos of the children while you have been in your new location. Now is the time to download them into individual small albums, one for each child. These albums can be stuffed in the airplane carry-on backpack. They are useful talking-time tools.

When you get home, or to your new location, keep these albums in an easy-to-reach place and notice how often your child looks at them. You will be looking for clues to monitor *other-home sickness* and get an idea of which children your child really misses.

Make a DVD of the house where you have been living. Our family had one special house in particular that we loved. Years later, we still bring this DVD out at some point over Christmas or on Mother's Day (for *my* fond memories!). If you are the creative sort, make a DVD of memories for each child.

Marlene, my walking partner I mentioned earlier, took her children and my children out for a day together to make our family a photo album of all the special-to-us-places in Ridgefield, where we were living at the time. Her children and mine were close friends, so this was a closure activity for them as well as enjoyed by us. You are blessed when you receive thoughtful closure presents.

Transition for Levels One and Two

You will have made regular trips back home and kept in contact with family, your church, and possibly even your children's school and classmates. Do not assume though, that you and your children will simply slip back into home life in the first few days. Re-entry at every level has its transition challenges.

Level One people often say that in a few short months it seems as if they have never been away, but your biggest surprise may be that no one—not family, not friends—wants to know about your time away. You will need to organize some formal ways for both you and your children to connect with the old neighborhood.

I suggest you have a word with your children's teachers and see if the kids can do at least a show and tell of where they have been living. If the kids are quite young, ask their Sunday School teacher if they can tell about their experiences of living overseas, and then have the class pray for the country where they have been living. This is the time to see if any other children at church have lived in foreign lands and get them together for a play date, afternoon tea, etc.

You may want to share a meal with another family from your church who has also lived overseas, and ask them to tell you about their experiences. Every time this has been done, families tell me that they end the meal by saying, "Thanks for listening—no one else would want to!"

Make a scrapbook before you leave. When you get back to your home country, set the scrapbook out on the coffee table; simply leave it there for visiting relatives and friends to glance at while you leave them alone for a minute or two. Several clients who have done this said it was amazing that family and friends who hadn't seemed to want to talk about their time away, suddenly brought the scrapbook into the kitchen and said, "What is this?" and then the stories began.

Let family and friends be the ones to bring up the subject of your time overseas, and show willingness to discuss your adventure. Do two things: give them something concrete like a scrapbook as a tool for knowing how to ask you questions, and reassure them that you are glad to be home. One more thing you can do: just as you had a good-bye party when you left, have a house re-warming when you come home. Tell everyone how much you missed him or her and celebrate the fact that you are back!

Also remember that almost no school back home looks like a national school overseas. Though you have minimized the transition issues to some degree, your children will still go through re-entry transition. Give your kids some extra mom and dad time, encouraging them to talk to you about their new school and anything they might miss about Hong Kong, London, or wherever you have been living.

Another note for Level Two families: you have probably enjoyed regular family weekend trips to discover the overseas country. I suggest that you continue this routine, only now within a home-style budget. Get the kids to do some research to see what is interesting in their own country—and go see it! You have a lot to do when you return home, but a once-a-month week-end away, even to stay with a relative, gives your family the feeling that they are still discovering new things together.

Note to teacher: Please write a note to the teacher on the very first day of school. Tell the teacher how excited (or not) your child is about "coming home." Remind them of the country where you have been living. Your child's teacher may not have had time to read your child's notes and as most Level One and Two children do not change their accents while living overseas, it will not be obvious that your child needs transition support. They will "sound like everyone else," and often their needs go unnoticed. Write another note at the end of the first week, thanking the teacher for all she or he has done to make your child feel welcomed in their home country. Continue to bring this "home to your teacher" until your child "feels at home."

TRANSITION FOR LEVEL THREE, FOUR, AND FIVE

When Level Three, Four, or Five families return to their home country, they often go to a new, more international location than one they may have called "home." You are not keen on cultural dominancy, even back home. You will most likely look for an international school for your children. Have a talk with the teachers at the new school, and ask them for advice on how best to transition your children into that school. International school teachers are trained in transition, and you can share the challenge of your move with them.

Take great care though, if you are moving from a Level Three, Four, or Five relocation lifestyle to a Level One or Two. Changing levels, if you are moving out of your personal comfort zone, can be as challenging as changing countries. Most teachers living a Level One or Two lifestyle themselves have no idea how to help a child who has been living a Level Three or Four international lifestyle. Too many times I have heard a home country teacher, who years ago had lived overseas, ignore the needs of an American child coming home. I have also seen a child who had been evacuated out of Pakistan and had spent some time in Dubai have to listen to a teacher cheerfully speak of the "wonderful time she had had in the Middle East" and "poo-pooed" any possible transition issues a child might have in these very different times.

If you are moving from Levels Three, Four, or Five to Levels One or Two relocation in your next country, seriously search out your local international community for support.

Take a good look at your church. Is it multinational? Are all races represented? Your Level Three and Four child will be more comfortable in these surroundings. If your children are attending a Level One school, they may especially enjoy some time in the week in which they can have Level Three moments.

When visiting your children's school, remember that we teachers are like mothers. You need to take care when you are criticizing our kids or our curriculum. Sometimes teachers can be quite sensitive when you announce that your child "already covered" a subject in "their last school." Approach any school curriculum adjustments you want for your child with courtesy. We have had older children tell a teacher that she "had covered that" when it turned out the student just didn't want to "do math" in any country!

Always write a note to the teacher on the first day of school and at the end of the first week of school, thanking them for their support in assisting your child make the transition from one country to another. You need to gently remind the teacher that your child needs her or his support at this time, especially in making new friends.

Awkward Level Four People

Awkward Level Four people are those who know that they are never going home. Though they may at some point try Level One living arrangements for a few months, they become irritable and difficult to live with. People who truly love international relocation are not going to give the right to any culture to tell them what to do or how to think or behave. These are people who consistently select a Level Four Relocation. They love the "heading out," but not the "heading home." If this is you and your corporation wants your family back at the ranch headquarters, ensure that you are moving to a Level Four location within that territory and enjoy. Watch for the next overseas assignment, and be ready to roll!

Changing Levels

Still, if you *are* heading out to a new country, changing levels is a good way of confirming which level you prefer. Just as changing levels can be difficult if you are moving out of your comfort zone, it can be the solution if you have not been blooming where you are planted.

If you are staying on a long-term overseas assignment and find that you are not happy, consider changing levels rather than just opting to go home. Sometimes it is not the country you are living in that is that is the problem, but in what level you are living in that country.

LEVEL SIX

As much as is possible, you have lived the life of the host country. You have learned a new dialect of English, if not a new language, and you have come to know the ways of another people. The transition back home will be made easier if you are able to plan a trip or two back to the host country. No one wants to think that they will never again see the place where they have enjoyed living. With a few close host country friends, plan vacations together and invite them to your country.

Level Six families often make life-long friends from the host country, and children grow up with a particular affiliation to their host country friends. Kids who attend a Level Six school can return to the host country and still see familiar people and old friends. Children who have lived a Level One to Five overseas life may return to the host country and find a familiar building but no one they know will be there. Often even the teachers in international schools will have moved on.

Easing Level Six Transition/Re-entry

If you move back to your country of origin, often called "re-entry," you may have a new sympathy for foreigners living in your community. One way of easing your re-entry time is to be part of your church's welcoming committee. Jesus made welcoming a priority; in Luke 9:11 it says that He welcomed the people, taught them, and healed the sick.

Anyone who has ever lived overseas will know how it feels to have a warm welcome to something new. As you think of others and offer them a welcome, you may find your own re-entry needs met.

At your children's schools, make an appointment and show the teacher(s) a scrapbook of your children's work. Be sensitive to appearing critical of your home country curriculum or sounding as if you think your child is now streets ahead of anyone his or her age. Recognize what your child has achieved, and be clear about the gaps in their education. They may now be ahead in reading, or math, but local history might need work. Ask the teacher if there are any family field trips you might make to help your child catch up with local knowledge.

At first family gatherings, keep an extra eye on the kids and give them something constructive to do. Recognize that cousins may not know what to say to each other at first, and organize a day at a fun park or something that will actively give them a shared experience. Tell you children to be sensitive and not to sound superior about their travels if they want to have any friends at the end of the day.

Level Seven

You aren't going home, so what do you care about transition to anywhere else?

The Strategy Summary

First of all, set your priorities. God is first in your life. He will guide you regarding the work He wants you to do and where He wants you to do it. Let Him guide you as to whether you should live among your own nationality while overseas, the international community, or focus on getting to know the host country.

Let your Level of Relocation be mission focused. Ask God to show the needs of the people who are also living at your level and ask Him for divine appointments. Be a worker in the harvest of your calling.

The second priority in your life is your family. Some members of your wider family will need to release you and your nuclear family to go to new places so that you can serve and live out God's purpose and plan for your life. Even if you can't speak the language in a new land, learn the love languages of your family members and know in "your knower" that you are loved and how you can love them. This is a love that travels well.

Let your Level of Relocation be ministry focused. Ask Father God for divine appointments to gather your personal support team and enable you to be part of His wider international family known as the Church. You are blessed to be a blessing.

The Third Priority—Friendship

This book has been about faith and family as you relocate overseas, but I end with the third priority—your friends. This is not a girly moment for friendship, though I value those friendships. This is not about men bonding to live out the Father heart of God, though that is crucial to the strength of our society. Other books have been written in more depth on friendship, and even friendship evangelism. My take on friendship is focused on appreciating those people who share your life journey, even if it is only for five hours of the 35-hour flight to Seoul.

Friends are indeed, forever, whether you have known them all your life or simply had a fleeting moment on an airplane. Friends have spirit-to-spirit conversations.

Let me explain, I cherish friends I have had for great lengths of time, but I also cherish someone who comes alongside me at those special times when I have needed direction.One friend I will always give thanks for is Anne Wright. She "happened" to come alongside me as a slightly older and wiser friend, offering encouragement, wisdom and friendship (and great stories of growing up as an American in Syria) when I was a young mother, pregnant and living overseas. I give thanks for people who I've known for a season (though Anne and I still email) and then are released to adventures in far-flung places. God says how long we get to have time with a friend.

Does this mean that anyone and everyone is a friend? Not at all. I have known people for over 30 years whom God may have called me to bless or from whom to receive blessings or just pass the time of day, but they are not necessarily my friends. For me, there is a spirit connection in friendship; something that says we are on a God-ordained journey; and if I only have five minutes with you, it is to encourage that journey.

The reason for friendship is to get to know Someone who is our only true Friend; the Friend who goes with us everywhere and sticks closer to us than a brother. That Friend is Jesus. That Friend gave His life for you, and He did it so that you could have a full life that glorifies Father God. I don't know about you, but I don't want to waste the time my Friend spent on the cross.

Anne Graham Lotz says in her book, *My Heart's Cry*,[2] that when she was speaking to a group of professional women golfers the night before the U.S. Women's Open, she was "struck by the intensity of their focus as they pursued their goal of competing in and winning the golf tournament. Their entire lives, including diet, schedules, activities, friendships and material resources, revolved around their one purpose—of being the best golfers they could be."

In her talk, she then told them that she "also had a similar sense of purpose that dictated where I went, how I spent my time and money, what I said and did, and who I interacted with."

Anne said, "Simply stated" her purpose in life "is to increasingly grow in my personal knowledge of God as I follow Him in a life of faith. I want to know God today better than I knew Him yesterday. I want to know Him better next year than I do this year. I want to know Him until one day, like Abraham, God refers to me as His friend!"

Freely we have received (passports, plane tickets, opportunities, food, water), freely may we give of whatever He gives us to give others. Today, let us entertain a stranger or two, and speak encouragement and life into the lives of others. As we go in Jesus' name, others will know that He lives.

Appendix A

FAMILY RELOCATION
LISTENING EXERCISES

In the following exercises, I have used the example of Nicky and Sila Lee in their excellent Marriage Preparation Course at Holy Trinity Brompton (Alpha International, © Nicky and Sila Lee; Brompton Road, SW7 1JA London, 2007). As part of a couple's preparation for marriage, they encourage Reflective Listening, which focuses on demonstrating that you have indeed heard what your fiancé has said. This type of listening is also a feature of their excellent *Marriage Book*; (www.htb.org).

Further and more extensive information on reflective listening can be obtained from the Acorn Foundation (www.acornchristian.org), in Borden, Hampshire, England, where there are courses that focus on developing the skill of purposeful listening. (Acorn in the UK has no relation to the political group in the U.S.A. Acorn UK is called Christian Healers in the U.S.A.) Rev. Dr. Russ Parker, Director of Acorn Healing Foundation, along with the Christian Listening team members, provide residential courses that include "Learning to Listen," "Called to Listen," and "Time to Listen," along with Quiet Days and teaching for specific emotional and physical healing needs. This group sends teams to war-torn areas to listen to people who have traveled dangerous and traumatic routes to the safety of refuge camps. For most of us, our concerns will be more about packing and leaving friends and family behind, yet it is a help to some to keep this perspective of those who will never see an airline ticket or enjoy short stays in a hotel while awaiting the furniture shipment. Sometimes it helps to keep this in mind when we are at the end of our patience with delayed flights.

EXERCISE 1

Over a meal or while traveling, ask each family member the following questions. The only rule is that you listen and do not interrupt while someone is speaking. When the speaker has finished what he or she wants to say, have someone in the family summarize what has been said. You may find it fun to have a child summarize what a parent has said, and a parent summarize what a child has said. Vary who gets to summarize, but in every case try to listen until the speaker has finished what he or she wants to say.

1. How do you feel when no one listens to you?*

2. How do you feel when someone listens to you?*

3. How do you feel when trying to listen to important information given in a foreign language?

*From the Acorn Christian Foundation, Whitehill Chase, Bordon, Hampshire, GU35 0AP.

EXERCISE 2

Place a small basket in the center of the table. Give each family member a sheet of paper and a pen, and ask them to write down a list of concerns they have about moving to your new location. When each person has had time to complete their list, have them select one concern in particular that they are happy to share. Write down that concern on a separate, small piece of paper without signing it. Fold it and put it in the basket.

Pass the basket around and have everyone pick one folded paper that they know is not their own. Have everyone guess who they think wrote the concern they selected and ask them to read it aloud (with respect). When family members guess correctly whose concern it was, ask the person who wrote it to say more about that concern. When the person has finished speaking, the person who pulled their paper from the basket will reflect on what they think they heard the person say. This is not counseling. You are not offering solutions, simply summarizing what you have heard.

When you have completed a summary, ask the person who wrote the concern, "Did I get all you were saying?" If yes, go to the next person who can then select a slip of paper from the basket. If no, listen again! Keep at it until you can summarize the concern to the satisfaction of the person who wrote it.

At the end of this exercise, you can agree to "go down the list of concerns," practicing listening and summarizing one concern at a time. You can do this all at once or select one concern per listening time. This is a good exercise for evenings you set aside as family listening nights. You can agree to complete these evenings with praying together for God to provide solutions for everyone's concerns. Remember to tell each other when you have received answers to prayer. Praise reports are encouraging!

EXERCISE 3

Ask each person what they are looking forward to with this relocation. You can vary this topic by asking each person to name a friend they are leaving behind, and to suggest any ideas they have for keeping in touch. You can also ask questions such as what sort of friend would you like in your new location, and what makes a good "new friend?"

EXERCISE 4

Let each member of the family reflect one at a time on how they feel about being "new"—the new kid on the playground, the new mom or dad in the neighborhood or office. Ask, "What is it about being new that you like, and don't like?"

Again, remember to listen until each speaker finishes what they have to say and take time to summarize that you have heard correctly. Pray for each other at the end of this exercise. Complete the exercise with family prayer time.

EXERCISE 5

Read through the Levels of Moving (Chapter 2) and give each person time to say which level they hope to make in this relocation, and why. Do not urge agreement with your own intended level of move. Just listen and reflect back on what you hear. At the end of the exercise, pray for Father God's leading for the level that is right for you and your family.

EXERCISE 6

Read through the Levels of Moving and pick one of the levels for your entire family. Ask each person to tell you how a move at this level would affect them, both positively and negatively. Remember to have someone summarize what they have heard each family member say, and remember also that you are just listening and not correcting or offering counseling.

Appendix B

RELOCATION LEVEL QUESTIONNAIRE

The following questionnaire is an aid to discussion, not a scientifically administered tool for research.

Please enjoy reviewing these questions and use them to help you begin to discover your level of relocation. This is not meant to be an academic study where the biases are noted and the answers collated. Nonetheless, these questions should serve to aid you and members of your family begin a discussion regarding how you intend to live in your new country.

Make a note of your answers to each question (you can have multiple answers as you go through the questionnaire) and then check the comments made at the very end.

1. Where are you from?

   a. You quickly name a single location (Levels 1, 2, and 7).

   b. You name a place of birth, and then add, "but I've lived in _____ for a long time." (Levels 1,2,3,4,5,6)

   c. You hate this question as you have lived so many places it is difficult to answer. You hope airlines will someday understand dual nationals and stop asking silly questions on arrival papers! (Levels 3,4,5,6,7)

   d. This is an easy question. You and your family have lived in _____ for a considerable length of time, and no matter how many times you go overseas, this is where you say you are "from" (however you define it!). Each member of your family may be from a different place of birth, but together you have developed an identity, even if it is a dual national identity. You can say, "We are American or we are Canadian, or we are French, or we are Irish-American, etc." (This has nothing to do with passports. See question below). (Levels 1,2,5,6.7)

Example: For this question, my answer is c, so I could be Levels 3,4,5,6,7)

Your answer is: _____. And you could be Levels

_____

2. Have you ever moved before? The answer to this question will determine your Experience Level of Moving, not the relocation level you are selecting for this move.

    a. No, this will be my first family move. (Level 1 Experience Level)

    b. Yes, I moved as a child but this is our first family move (Level 2 Experience Level).

    c. Yes, I have moved with my family but never as far as our new location. (Level 2 Experience Level)

    d. Yes, I have moved overseas once (or twice?) before (from short-term to long-term). (Level 3 Experience Level)

    e. Yes! I've moved overseas so many times we've just about lost count! We have not been relocating for many years, but we have been to a considerable number of places in the past few years. Let's see, there was Hong Kong...no that was when Emily was little, oh and Daniel born in... (Level 4)

    f. Yes, I've lived a long time (more than 10 years) overseas and in a couple of countries (not the 5 moves in 4 years life!) (Level 4)

g. I was a global nomadic kid and now with my family we just keep on moving! (Level 5)

Example: My answer is f, as I have lived in three different countries (OK, several different locations in one of those countries), but for a significant length of time in each location. So my level of experience is 4.

You may be getting married to someone from another country and relocating to that country at a Level 6 or 7, but your experience level is a 1 (never moved), 2 (moved locally or you moved once or twice as a child but not as an adult with your own family), 3 (moved one or twice internationally), 4 (considerable number of moves within a short number of years, or many years overseas in a small number of locations), or 5 (life-long global nomad).

For this question, your answer is _____. You could be Levels _____

Circle this answer. Check whether the answer to this question, your Level of Experience in relocation, matches your Level of Relocation for your next move.

3. Does everyone in your family have the same passport?

    a. We all have the same passport. (Level 1)

    b. We all have the same passport, but one or two of us have/has an additional passport/s. (Levels 2, 3,4,5,6,7)

    c. I have one passport and my spouse has another passport. We are a two-passport family. (The children may have dual nationality.) (Levels 2,3,4,5,6,7)

    d. Hmmm. We've stuffed so many passports in our travel bags that we have to figure out which ones we are using at the moment. We are a multiple-passport family. (Levels 3,4,5,6)

For example, we have quite a number of passports in my family, but as my husband and I each have a single passport, we are a two-passport family. Cousins, nieces and nephews have a variety of passports, but I will let them select option d. For me, I answer with option c, which gives me Levels 2,3,4,5,6,7)

For this question, you are option _____. Your Levels could be _____

4. How long do you intend to be here?

    a. Short assignment of less than a year (any Level)

    b. One to two year assignment (any Level)

    c. Three to seven year assignment (any Level)

    d. Who knows? (Level 4 or 5)

    e. Forever (Level 6 or Level 7)

For this question, I could be Levels _____

For example, my husband and I travel back and forth at the moment spending half a year in one country and half in another, so I have selected option d for my answer, which gives me Level 4 or 5.

Your option _____, which could be Levels _____ or _____

5. What type of curriculum are you interested in for your children?

    a. I would like my children to have their home country curriculum (as much as possible) (Level 1 or 2)

    b. I would like my children to study for the international baccalaureate (Level 3,4,5)

    c. I would like my children to study the host country (new location) curriculum (Level 6 or 7)

    d. Other _____ (for example, home
      schooling) (Level 1)

For this question I could be Levels _____

For example, I selected option c for my children, which gives me a Level 6 or 7.

Your option is _____, which gives you Levels _____

6. What are your long-term family education goals?

    a. I hope the kids will want to head back home to attend training, college, or work (Level 1,2,3)

    b. I hope the kids will decide to look at a variety of choices and attend higher education or training anywhere in the world (Level 3,4,5)

    c. I hope the kids will at least consider attending higher education or training in our new host country (Level 6 or 7)

    d. Other _____

For example, I selected option b, which gives me Levels 3,4,5. I may have raised them with host country curriculum, but hoped they would choose from a world of options. It should come as no surprise that they carried on with host country education, but traveled widely as a supplement to their education.

For this question you are _____, which gives you Levels _____

7. Do you have any faith-based preferences for selecting a school?

Note: This question needs to be asked before you relocate, but people of the same faith often select different levels of living in a new community, depending on their purpose for relocation. Make a note of your answer and then see how it impacts your Level of Living.

  a. Yes, and I would like the children to attend a faith-based school or to home school in a particular faith.

  b. Yes, but I am happy for the children to attend a school of another denomination of the Christian faith, or a Jewish school of a different congregation, for example.

  c. Yes, but am happy to compromise and have the children attend a secular school as long as the standards of education are good and their beliefs are respected.

  d. No, they need to know how to live their faith in a secular world.

  e. No, we have no faith-based preferences for selecting a school.

For this question you are _____. The answer may or may not affect your Level of Relocation, but it is important to have clarity on this subject. Listen and do not judge each other's answers. It is a topic for prayer.

Note: You may have a different response depending on the ages of your children. For example, I answered "a" when my children were in elementary school as I wanted them grounded in Christian education, but was prepared to answer "d" when they were older and needed to practice living out their faith in a secular world before heading off to college. On one overseas move, there was no faith-based school choice available; but in clarifying my preferences, I could make up at home what they lacked at school.

8. If you have a dinner party in your new location, you would be most comfortable inviting…

  a. Only people from my own country living in the new location. (Level 1)

b. Mostly my own nationality, but would include others who have lived in (and loved) my country. (Level 2)

c. A variety of nationalities. The more the merrier! (Level 3 or 4)

d. The local people. I would invite the locals! (Levels 5,6,7)

The dinner party test! For example, I selected option c and that puts me happily in a Level 3 or 4 for relocation.

For this question, I am Levels _____

9. What sort of travel do you hope to do while living in your new location?

a. Not much, maybe just look around the neighborhood (see some local sites). If I travel anywhere it will be back home to see family and to shop. (Level 1)

b. I want to see everything there is to see in our new location, and that means the entire country if possible on our budget! (Level 2)

c. I want to have time to see this new region of the world. (Level 3,4,5,6,7)

d. Wherever I am living has little impact on where I travel. I go anywhere! (Level 4)

For example, I have selected option d as I love to travel and where I live has no bearing on my travel plans. Living with an international community means I am often tempted to visit a range of international invitations!

For this question you are Levels _____

10. What type/amount of communication are you hoping for from your children's new school?

a. I would like our new school to match our home country school in type and amount of communication. (Levels 1 and 2)

b. I know we will need to adapt to our host country's ways and means of teachers communicating with parents. (Levels 3,4,5)

c. We have moved around so much that we no longer have a communication preference, as long as my kids are happy and do well in school. (Levels 3,4,5)

d. I have a preference as to how a school communicates with parents, but I am willing to work with teachers to get this right for my kids. (Levels 3,4,5,6,7)

For example, I selected option d, and it was work to get good communication!

For this question you selected option _____, which gives you Levels _____

11. From what you know at the moment, how much of the new location culture (in this case, culture simply means the customs and ways of living, not whether they prefer Sibelius over Grieg) do you want to adopt into your own or your family's lifestyle?

a. We will stay behind the gates of our house and keep the host country culture out as much as possible! (Level 1)

b. I am curious as to how the people in our host country live, but will be guided by other expats from my home country regarding adapting to local customs. I may or may not learn the new language. (Level 2)

c. I look forward to learning about host country food, mixing with the locals, and learning from them how they live. I will take a stab at learning the new language. Who knows, I could become fluent! (Levels 3,4,5)

d. I want to become a host country local! I want to be fluent in the new language! (Levels 6,7)

For this question I am Levels _____

For example, I selected option c as I enjoy each new location for the potential opportunities for learning new things. This option gives me Levels 3,4,5

You select option _____, which gives you Levels _____

12. From what you know at the moment, how much of the new location parenting style do you want to adapt into your own family's lifestyle?

a. None! They believe kids should be seen and not heard and that bedtimes are sacred. That won't fit in with our way of doing things. (Level 1 or 2)

b. Some, I suppose. We know we will need to adapt to their way of (for example) keeping the kids up late when you have friends over for dinner or if you go to a restaurant, but I hope to continue with some of my home country ways of raising kids. (Levels 3,4,5)

c. I prefer their way of raising kids and so glad to not be in our home country in this stage of my children's lives. (Levels 6,7)

d. I intend to raise our kids with our own standards, and it is not a matter of a country's culture. Some of our principles fit easier into one culture and others into another country's customs. Wherever we live we will not be conforming to this world. (Levels 1,2,3,4,5,6)

For example, I often selected b. Sometimes it worked and sometimes it didn't.

You choose, for this particular move _____, and this gives you Levels _____

Comments: Write down how many times you answer one of the above questions with each particular Level. Are you mostly a Level 1 or 2? Or mostly Levels 3,4,5? Or mostly Levels 6 or 7? Go back over the Level Descriptions in Chapter 2 to narrow down the possibilities.

From my answers, you can see that I am an Experience Level 4, who has Level 3,4,5 preferences for relocation. For family reasons, I needed to live a Level 6 life for a while, but when I changed the level of living to Level 4, my quality of life improved greatly. It is cheaper to change levels than country, and often changing your country does not solve lifestyle issues. If you are, or are about to be a global nomad, take time to consider the level of living in another culture that is best for you, and best for your family.

If, after taking this little questionnaire, you see that certain members of your family are intending to make a different level of move than the level you prefer, you know you have things to discuss! Practice reflective listening, pray for God's guidance, and work together to move together.

Decide on a level of living before you need to make any actual choices regarding housing or school selection and see just how comfortable you are with the possibility of living out your relocation assignment at that level. I liken it to wearing a coat. "Put on a level and wear it for a few days" to see how you feel. Do you wake up in the middle of the night thinking, "No way! I could never adapt to that. It's just not a good fit!" or is there a peace that says, for example, "Yes, in my spirit, I just know I could happily live a Level Two life when we move to _____."

Appendix C

SAMPLE SCHOOL VISIT SCHEDULE

Visiting Schools for (Child):

Temporary Accommodation: **Contact Number:**

Education Consultant: **Mobile Number:**

Driver: **Mobile Number:**

Other: **Mobile Number:**

Date	Meeting and Pick Up
Time	First School Visit: Address, telephone number and contact name
Time	Second School Visit
Time	Third School Visit
Day Two	
Time	First School Visit
Time	Second School Visit
Time	Third School Visit

Notes on School Reports

Appendix D

SCHOOL VISIT STRENGTHS AND WEAKNESSES CHART

School	Strengths	Weaknesses
1.		
2.		
3.		
4.		
5.		
6.		

Appendix E

ACE CHECKLIST

ACADEMICS

The academic style at _____ school is:

- ❏ Traditional

- ❏ Contemporary

- ❏ Alternative

The academic type of program at _____ school is:

- ❏ Home Country

- ❏ International Baccalaureate

- ❏ Host Country

- ❏ Special Needs (Type _____)

For me, the features of this school are: _____

For me, the challenges of this school are: _____

What is the push/pressure level at this school?

- ❏ Just right for my child

- ❏ A little too much/too little, but my child could handle it

- ❏ Not appropriate for my child/our family

Where is the spark? _____

Does the school have a teacher who understands academic transition?

COMMUNICATION

What is the communication style of this school? _____

Can I work with this style of communication? _____

How much notice will I get that my child needs me to make a costume for a school play? _____

ENVIRONMENTAL

Does this school's environment nurture my child? _____

Is the staff dedicated to making this school a physically and emotionally safe place for my child to learn? _____

Do we like the uniform? No uniform? _____

Appendix F

SUPPORT TEAM CONTACT INFORMATION

Heavenly Father: And the peace of God, which transcends all under-standing, will guard your hearts and your minds in Christ Jesus (Philippians 4:7).

Prayer Partner: _____

Health Advisor: _____

Bible Study Group: _____

Education: _____

Driver: _____

Housing: _____

Finance: _____

Time-off: _____

Food: _____

Others: _____

Endnotes*

*All of the Websites listed are accessible as of the writing of this book. Apologies if any have been relocated or removed between the time of writing and reading.

Preface

1. *Global Relocation Trends 2009 Report*, 2009 Brookfield Global Relocation Services, page 8. Note: previously known as the GMAC Relocation Services, Global Relocation Trends Survey; rebranded in 2009. This report, in conjunction with the U.S. National Foreign Trade Council, is the international benchmark report for worldwide expatriate services. You can download this report in full from the excellent Website (www.brookfieldgrs.com) and also review the Country Club Series. This series offers a one-hour Webinar, focusing on cultural communication for a featured country (every other month).

2. *Global Relocation Trends 2008*, "Finding suitable Candidates, Early Returns from Assignments and Attrition," page 9.

3. For further discussion regarding Return on Investment (ROI) and the difficulties in defining assignment ROI, please note page 13 of the 2009 *Brookfield Global Relocation Services*. For the purposes of *Parents on the Move!* the word *failure* is used when referring to a work assignment that ends before the assignment has been successfully completed to the originally agreed upon standards. Each company will have its own standard for success, and many may wish to use the term "Early

Return" rather than label an assignment a failure. My focus is on enabling parents to successfully meet their goals for a thriving family life while supporting the parent who is on work assignment.

INTRODUCTION

1. *2009 Global Relocation Trends 2009 Report*, Brookfield Global Relocation Services, page 16.

CHAPTER 1: STRATEGIC PRIORITIES

1. *2009 Global Relocation Trends Survey Report*, Brookfield Global Relocation Services (in association with the USA National Foreign Trade Council), page 17.
2008 Global Relocation Trends Survey (GRTS) GMAC, page 9; and Expatlanidia.com (for up-to-date articles concerning this research).

CHAPTER 2: SEVEN LEVELS OF MOVING

1. The following recommended reading list is quite comprehensive. It may not be possible to read all as you prepare to relocate, but if you can only read a few, start at the top and make your way down the list.

Before you go:

D. Pollock and R. Van Reken, *Third Culture Kids: Growing Up Among Worlds* (Boston: Intercultural Press, 1999).

Susan Miller, *But Mom, I Don't Want To Move!: Easing the Impact of Moving on Your Children* (Colorado Springs, CO: Focus on the Family Publishing, 2004).

For teens and pre-teens:

Beverly D. Roman, *Footsteps Around the World* (Jacksonville, FL: BR Anchor Publishing, 2007; Teens, Revised edition 2008). *The League of Super Movers* (BR Anchor Publishing Preteens, Revised edition).

Anything and everything written by Robin Pascoe, including:

Robin Pascoe, *Raising Global Nomads: Parenting Abroad in an On-Demand World* (Piet-Pelon, NJ: Expatriate Press Limited, 2006).

Robin Pascoe, *A Moveable Marriage: Relocate Your Relationship without Breaking It* (Piet-Pelon, NJ: Expatriate Press Limited, 2003).

Robin Pascoe, Surviving Overseas: *The Wife's Guide to Successfully Living Abroad* (Times Books International, 1992).

Robin Pascoe, *Culture Shock! Successful Living Abroad—A Parent's Guide* (Times Books International, 1994).

Jo Parfitt, *A Career in Your Suitcase* (North Vancouver, British Columbia: Summertime Publishing, 2008).

When the plane lands (though these books can be great preparation books as well):

Susan Miller resources as noted in the Website list below.

Joyce Bowers, *Raising Resilient MKs: Resources for Caregivers, Parents, and Teachers* (Colorado Springs, CO: Association of Christian Schools International, 1998).

Janet Feitsort, *Long Distance Grandma* (Brentwood, TN: Howard Publishing Company, 2005).

Peter Gosling, Anne Huscroft with Jo Parfitt, *How to be a Global Grandparent* (United Kingdom: Zodiak Publishing, 2009).

Worth reading before you go but essential for re-entry:

Robin Pascoe, Homeward Bound, *A Spouse's Guide to Repatriation* (Piet-Pelon, NJ: Expatriate Press, 2000).

Jill Crystal PhD and Liz Perelstein, MA, *A 'How to Guide' for Repatriation* (White Plains, NY: School Choice International, 2007).

Neal Pirolo, *The Reentry Team: Caring for Your Returning Missionaries* (San Diego, CA: Emmaus Road International, 2000).

www.transitionallearning.com – Helpful Website or assistance to military families.

Places to purchase excellent materials to help prepare children for relocation.

> www.figt.com – Families in Global Transition, the foremost resource for missionary, military, diplomatic and corporate relocation and family life.

> www.ocfusa.org – Military Officers' Christian Fellowship.

> www.tckworld.com – Third Culture Kids.

> www.justmoved.org – For raising global kids! This Website is for children, teens, and parents alike; Susan Miller is founder and president of Just Moved! Ministries.

2. Note: my son Mark loves both of his countries. He is equally at home in the USA and the UK yet he says he always feels more English when he is in America and more American when he is in England.

3. Report on the findings of the joint ExpatExpert.com and AMJ Campbell International Relocation Survey. "Family Matters" International Relocation Survey by Expat Expert/AMS Campbell © September 2008 states that "66.7 % of respondents noted that a child's education (desires not met) was a reason for assignment failure. www.expatexpert.com; page 10.

4. "Slightly out of place" is my own expression based on anecdotal evidence in my own family and in working with dual and multinational children. One of the best resources for this is www.tckworld.com.

5. Pierrepont is part of Ellel Ministries International. See the Website at www.ellel.org.

CHAPTER 3: CHECKING OUT THE GIANTS

1. Church locator Website: www.findachurch.com. This Website is a start, but the best Website, in my opinion, is yet to be built. I still google the town/city and search under "churches" or "synagogues."

CHAPTER 5: THE HOME SCHOOLING OPTION

1. It is difficult to categorize home schooling resources into those that are for short periods of time and those for the long haul, but the ones

I have listed here are amenable to selecting a class or two and you do not need to sign up for the whole curriculum. Other home schooling curricula (as listed in Endnote 3) may also allow for this, but they are often recommended for families that choose to home school full time.

www.coreknowledge.com – This is a good website if you would like to know what teachers in the public schools consider standards of excellence for K-12, including lesson plans.

www.abeka.com – This site gives you curriculum kits and other resources for nursery through twelfth grade Christian education, including downloadable progress reports. Many families have used this curricula full time, or ordered a subject or two as they could afford them.

www.aophomeschooling.com – This Christian home school Website offers a variety of curricula, including Switched On School House.

www.homeschools.org – This is the Christian Liberty Academy School System, better known as CLASS. This site helps you pull together a subject list using a variety of home school resources.

The following three magazines could be invaluable for getting started with home schooling:

www.teachinghome.com – This is the site of *The Teaching Home Magazine* and gives you tips for getting started.

www.thehomeschoolmagazine.com – This is the site of *The Old School House* magazine, which has to be one of the most attractive home school sites, in my opinion. There is a useful section for home schooling children with special needs.

www.homeschooljournal.net – This is an award-winning site for Jewish home schooling. Excellent recipes and lesson ideas for Jewish holidays.

2. More Websites to assist the home schooling parent:

www.education-otherwise.org – This British site has an excellent video to introduce you to home schooling possibilities. Remember if you are home schooling, you can think globally!

www.flora.org – This is an informational Website for Canadian home schooling, formerly known as the Canadian Homeschooling Resource page.

www.k12.com – This is often the online learning of choice provided by U.S. Public School System for virtual learning.

www.thesouthernbaptistacademy.org – This is a school without walls and is an accredited Christian academy. Take a look at the excellent blog written by the principal.

www.calvertschool.org – This home-based school has been going for over 100 years.

www.catholichomeschool.org – The Catholic Home School Site, offering a variety of curricula for Catholic families.

www.simplycharlottemason.com – Mrs. Mason (British) was born in the late 1800s, and her method is still famous with home schoolers. This site guides you through her methodology.

www.home-school.com – This is a good, practical site (The official site of *Practical Homeschooling* magazine with a blog for international home schoolers) for connecting with other home schoolers when you are relocating overseas; however, it doesn't mention Italy, so I am adding www.homeschoolcentral.com for a blog about home schooling in Italy.

www.homeschoolcentral.com – See previous description.

www.myhomeschoolingweb.com – for South Africa.

www.alloexpat.com – Also has forums where you can find home schooling parents in other parts of Africa and Asia.

www.imb.org – Where you will find a missionary in Kenya talking about setting up a resource site for home schoolers.

3. www.calvertschool.org – This home-based school has been going for over 100 years.

CHAPTER 6: YOUR SUPPORT TEAM—DO YOU HAVE ONE?

1. www.fivelovelanguages.com – This Website is a great introduction to Gary Chapman's work on learning to speak your spouse's language of loving and receiving love.

2. Robin Pascoe, *Homeward Bound. A Spouse's Guide to Repatriation* (Piet-Pelon, NJ: Expatriate Press Ltd., 2000). Check out Robin's site at: www.Expatexpert.com. As a "diplomatic wife," Robin is a well-known author and speaker on global nomadic family life.

3. www.deliaonline.com – This is the excellent Delia Smith Website.

   www.verybestbaking.com – Has the all-important Toll House Chocolate Chip Cookie recipe.

   www.bhg.com – Better Homes and Gardens Website.

   www.pbs.org/juliachild –This site shows videos of Julie Child demonstrating her famous cooking lessons.

CHAPTER 7: GRANDMOTHERS AS COMMUNICATION CENTRAL

1. *Global Relocation Trends, 2009 Survey Report*, Brookfield Global Relocation Services (in association with the USA National Foreign Trade Council), pages 8,15.

CHAPTER 8: EXPECTING AND DELIVERING A BABY ABROAD

1. Though I first heard this remark from a friend, I have since read it on several blogs about having babies overseas. Check out the Websites listed in this chapter to read the experiences of even more women who have given birth far from home.

2. The following are Websites to help you research about having a baby abroad. Please note that not every aspect of every Website aligns itself with Judaic-Christian principles.

   www.justmoms.com

   www.christian-mommies.com

   www.mothering.com

   www.thechristianwoman.com

www.expatwomen.com (click on Women Like You on left sidebar and then on "Mothers").

3. See the Websites above and Dr. Anne Copeland's book, *Global Baby, Tips to keep you and your Infant Smiling Before, During and After Your International Move* (Interchange Institute, 2004); www.interchangein-stitute.com.

4. www.llli.org – La Leche League International; a fabulous Website for breastfeeding support and information.

5. www.babycenter.org – For information on sleep, as well as other baby development topics. For a unique approach to raising children, visit: www.gentlechristianmothers.com.

6. www.fivelovelanguages.com – This Website is a great introduction to Gary Chapman's work on learning to speak your spouse's language of loving and receiving love. The book is excellent!

Chapter 9: Heading Home—Heading Out Again

1. www.transitionallearning.com – This is where you can purchase excellent materials to help you prepare your children for relocation or re-entry.

2. Anne Graham Lotz, My Heart's Cry (Nashville, TN: W Publishing Group, a Division of Thomas Nelson, Inc., 2002). Anne has re-released this book with a new title and devotional features called *Pursuing More of Jesus*; www.annegrahamlotz.com.

About the Author

For over 30 years, Kathleen McAnear Smith has lived and worked as a teacher overseas. She was born and raised in Washington, DC and continued her education at Stetson University in Florida, the School of International Service at American University, and a winter term at the University of Moscow. Kathleen also served as a Peace Corps Volunteer and high school teacher in Jamaica.

Since 1976, Kathleen relocated to five areas of the United Kingdom, experiencing re-entry to the United States and then returned to England, where she raised her daughter and son. During this time, she achieved an MSc in Social Policy at the University of Southampton, taught school, and created her own successful consulting business, Childtrack UK Ltd., which became internationally recognized by the CNN Business Traveller program in 2004. Childtrack specialized in relocating families primarily in the financial sectors of London and New York, with families coming in from all over the world.

As a follower of Jesus Christ, Kathleen has a heart for global family life, based on being raised in a missionary family, and believes that mature and wiser women have a vital role to play in assisting today's corporate women and men in the international arena.

For more information about this topic, please visit:

www.parentsonthemove.com

Additional copies of this book and other book
titles from DESTINY IMAGE™ EUROPE
are available at your local bookstore.

We are adding new titles every month!

To view our complete catalog online, visit us at:
www.eurodestinyimage.com

Send a request for a catalog to:

Via Acquacorrente, 6
65123 - Pescara - ITALY
Tel. +39 085 4716623 - Fax +39 085 9431270

"Changing the world, one book at a time."

Are you an author?

Do you have a "today" God-given message?

CONTACT US

We will be happy to review your manuscript
for the possibility of publication:

publisher@eurodestinyimage.com
http://www.eurodestinyimage.com/pages/AuthorsAppForm.htm